A Little Handbook for Volunteers

Anyone considering volunteering for a board of directors or currently serving on one will appreciate Dr. Freund's practical problem-solving strategies, gained from over 30 years of volunteer experience which she aptly calls, "holy work."

A Little Handbook for Volunteers

Lessons I Learned from Sister Gwendolyn

Dr. Annette S. Freund

authorHOUSE®

AuthorHouse™
1663 Liberty Drive
Bloomington, IN 47403
www.authorhouse.com
Phone: 1-800-839-8640

Published by AuthorHouse   10/07/2014

ISBN: 978-1-4969-4154-1 (sc)
ISBN: 978-1-4969-4153-4 (e)

Library of Congress Control Number: 2014916963

TABLE OF CONTENTS

Chapter 3: Leadership

Chapter 4: Moral Courage

Chapter 5: Change

Chapter 6:   Accountability

Chapter 7:   Appreciation

Chapter 8:   Conflict Resolution

Chapter 9: Committees

Lesson 9: Committee responsibilities must be clear, fair, and reasonable

Chapter 10: Feedback

Lesson 10: Boards must invite feedback to improve performance

PREFACE

Let's be honest. If you've ever served on a volunteer Board of Directors, you've probably experienced the best and worst of human behavior which, as you know, can be good, bad, and darn right ugly! For the past 30 years, I've served on numerous volunteer boards — from university advisory boards to non-profit boards of directors. During this time, I've met some of the finest, most dedicated people in the world. I've also seen some of the worst organizational leaders on the planet — and learned from their mistakes.

- Are you thinking about joining a volunteer board but aren't sure whether or not to make the commitment?
- Are you currently serving on a board but uncertain whether or not to continue?
- Are you leading a volunteer board but experiencing organizational difficulties?
- Are you a member of a board that seems to be falling apart?

The aim of this book is to provide practical advice to volunteers serving on boards. With so many activities competing for people's time, it's getting harder and harder to find qualified volunteers to do anything, yet alone commit to serving on a board. And once you've made the commitment, the last thing you want is to have your board fall apart. I know firsthand how devastating this can be. Each of the ten chapters contained herein contains a lesson I've learned while serving on boards — lessons that I hope can save your board time, frustration, and failure. I hope you will be able to apply the lessons I've learned to your board situation and use this "little handbook" as a reference tool to consult when board issues arise.

The idea for developing the book came while writing a white paper on the subject.[1] As the paper developed, it became quite clear to me that I had sufficient experience — both positive and negative — to write more extensively on the subject. I wrote the white paper just as my three-year term was about to expire on a volunteer board, an appointment I was honored to accept and reluctant to leave. If your term is about to expire, you may find my experiences in this book quite helpful, especially *Chapter 4: Board members must demonstrate moral courage* — the courage to take action for moral reasons despite the adverse consequences. I have learned that the best volunteer boards are those whose members aren't afraid to speak up and, when presented with unethical behavior, have the moral courage to take action, even if that action means leaving their seat on the board so as not to compromise their ethics.

Like yours, my ethics and understanding of volunteerism have been shaped by many people. I grew up in a home with two parents and 12 siblings in Bismarck, North Dakota. We had lots of responsibilities, lots of fun, lots of relatives, and lots of love. Since my birth order was 10th of 13, I benefited from lots of experience with siblings and a clear understanding of the value of teamwork. In addition, all 13 of us went to Catholic schools taught by the Benedictine Sisters of Annunciation Monastery in Bismarck, North Dakota, who mentored me through 16 years of elementary school, high school, and college. No one has had a more positive impact on my life, my ethics, my career, or my understanding of contributed services than these nuns who, by their example, taught me that volunteering truly is holy work.

I want to begin by thanking them, especially Sister Gwendolyn Pattock, OSB, who was an early mentor, teacher, role model, and inspiration. She was a Benedictine monastic attracted to divine goodness and beauty, finding it imaged in music, in flowers, and in the faces of children. A versatile and dedicated religious woman, she spent a half-century in pediatric nursing. Later she served as a mental health consultant and alumni director, then as assistant to the president of the University of Mary in Bismarck, North Dakota. She died in 2005 at the age of 93.

---

[1]   Annette S. Freund, "Why Volunteer Boards Fall Apart: Ten Lessons Learned in the Trenches," 2013.

Thanks also to my deceased parents and all my siblings from whom I learned the greatest lesson any volunteer can learn: "Example is not the main thing in influencing others. It is the only thing" (Albert Schweitzer).

I'm grateful also to friends and colleagues who read early drafts of my book proposal and encouraged me to write more: Anne Lawler, Peter Fenzel, Erenay Jackson, and Len Prazych, a long-time friend and Freund Associate, whose publishing experience has proven invaluable to me. Special thanks to my husband, John Freund — my soul mate, my supporter, and my biggest fan.

Finally, I want to express my sincere gratitude to all my fellow volunteers spread across this great land — from North Dakota to New Jersey. You have taught me that volunteerism is work that benefits others and not yourself, and that to volunteer you must put yourself and your ego aside. You are living proof that volunteerism is holy work.

CHAPTER 1

Mission

"I don't know what your destiny will be, but one thing I know: the only ones among you who will be really happy are those who have sought and found how to serve."

--Albert Schweitzer

Lesson 1: Every Board needs a clear mission, purpose, history, and vision

Before you raise your hand to serve on the board, ask to see its mission statement. Look for it on the first page of the organization's bylaws or website. If it doesn't have a mission statement, abandon all hope for this board. If it has one, then find out if it's being followed. Ask a few board members if they know what it says. If they can't articulate the mission or purpose, then very likely they're not following it. Don't even think of joining a board if the organization doesn't know why it exists, where it's been, or worse, doesn't care where it's going! The leaders are likely to have a "hidden agenda" or vision that differs from your own. Find another place to volunteer.

Case 1A: Shooting for the Stars

When I was in my 20s, I was hired as a part-time English instructor at my alma mater, the University of Mary in Bismarck, North Dakota, formerly Mary College. One day Sister Gwendolyn, the newly appointed Alumni Director, called me into her office to ask if I'd like to help establish the college's first-ever Alumni Association. It needed bylaws, a mission statement, policies, procedures, and officers, of course. It needed someone to help plan, organize, and develop these documents. It was her next question which surprised me, "Would you please serve as Acting President until the board gets established?" How could I refuse a nun? How could I refuse the pediatric nurse who knew my parents and the Schneider family, the one with "all those children"? Answer: I could not.

For several months, we worked on drafts of the documents. At each meeting, Sister Gwendolyn lit a votive candle and said a prayer for guidance. I'm sure she had no idea how much influence she was having on my life, yet alone in helping to formulate my understanding of and appreciation for volunteers. It was Sister Gwendolyn who showed me that volunteering really was holy work, and it set the tone for all my future volunteer activities.

By spring, we had drafted all the documents we needed to launch our new Alumni Association. By summer, the Board officially elected me President, and we were holding our first Alumni Reunions. Through all of it, Sister Gwendolyn demonstrated several qualities I admire in leaders of volunteer organizations:

- She understood that there is enormous, untapped kindness available from well-meaning, would-be volunteers who yearn for greater fulfillment through helping others.
- She knew how to tap the talents of these well-meaning volunteers *without exploiting them.* To do this, I noticed how she praised her volunteers publicly and often. She also wrote them personal "thank you notes," handwritten on note cards inscribed with this motivational quote from Robert Browning: "A man's reach should exceed his grasp, or what's a heaven for?" Like Browning, Sister Gwendolyn believed that our fledgling organization should shoot for the stars, soar, and tackle the unknown, regardless of fear. The soaring eagle on the front of the card was an apt image for what we were doing.
- She acknowledged every donation with a personal note and never let a good deed go unnoticed — from the kitchen help at alumni events to the cleanup crew. She demonstrated that if you want to motivate volunteers, you've got to know their individual talents, engage them in meaningful ways, and let them know their gifts of

time, talent, and treasure are sincerely appreciated, no matter how insignificant they may think their contributions are.

- She understood that organizations and their structures must adapt to changes in membership. Currently, the University of Mary Alumni Committee is the organization's advisory board. It evolved by a process of expansion from a seven-member Executive Board to a fifteen-member alumni council in November 1977. In December 1980, the membership was changed from fifteen to twelve, and in September 1991, the by-laws were again changed so that the membership consists of twelve to fifteen members. In 2011, the structure of the council was revised to its current advisory committee status.

According to the present website: "The goals of the Alumni Committee are to promote the interest and welfare of the alumni association; to foster the welfare and growth of the University of Mary; and to establish mutually beneficial relations between the university, students, faculty, parents, friends and its alumni."[2]

Not only does the organization have a clear statement of purpose, mission, and vision, but it also has a history of its evolution, including key dates, milestones, and even the names of every former Council Member, including mine.[3] Why is this important? Answer: Because an organization (or an individual for that matter) cannot know who they are unless they know where they've been. Clearly, Sister Gwendolyn and her successors understood this and kept good records. The importance of keeping records becomes obvious when you start trying to raise funds or establish credibility for your organization in the community. Your past affects your present. If your organization hasn't at least written down key milestones, get on it.

---

[2]   "Alumni Association: Current Committee Members," *University of Mary*, n. d., <http://www.umary.edu/alumni/association/council_tab1.php>.

[3]   "Alumni Association: Former Council Members," *University of Mary*, n. d., <http://www.umary.edu/alumni/association/council_tab2.php>.

Case 1B: Clarifying Your Purpose

Recently I was asked to volunteer for a small political organization. I hesitated because I was already involved in a number of other volunteer activities. Nevertheless, I agreed to offer what little free time I had to help set up before the meeting and take down afterwards. When I realized that I had never seen the mission statement of the organization, I started researching similar political organizations, hoping one of them would shed light on the mission of this one. The process led me to discover many good mission statements, which I thought could be adapted and customized for this organization. Here are some examples:

Example A: "The mission of this organization is to foster good government in our city, to encourage participation in their government by all citizens, and to make government responsive to the needs and objectives of its citizens. Also, to foster economic policies that provide adequate services for the city's citizens without jeopardizing the economic health of the city and that encourages reasonable development that enhances the city's image. And to promote and support the most qualified candidates for public office and appointed positions on City Agencies, Commissions, Committees, and Boards who support our mission."

Example B: "This organization serves as a forum for the exchange of political ideas and values, and to foster a sense of community among members who share these political views."

Example C: "Founded in 1911, this political organization has a rich history of advocacy. Our leadership works to ensure that the organization remains active and influential."

To write a good vision statement, think about how you would like to appear to the outside world for years to come. Understanding your goals and being able to state them clearly is the first step toward making them happen.[4] Although vision statements are meant as a roadmap for the future, they have the added value of helping you assess your progress toward the state your organization wishes to achieve. For this reason, your vision

---

[4] "Best Examples of a Vision Statement," *Your Dictionary*, 2014, <http://examples.yourdictionary.com/examples/best-examples-of-a-vision-statement.html>.

statement is worth posting on your website and communicating clearly and often to every member of your board.

Case 1C: Hidden Political Agendas

Have you ever been asked to serve on a board but knew little, if anything, about its mission? I have. Since I owned a small business, a business colleague invited me to lend a hand. What interested me most about this volunteer board was that it was concerned with finding people jobs and, since we were in an economic recession, this seemed to be an honorable cause — a "holy work," as Sister Gwendolyn might say. I accepted a three-year term and truly enjoyed the camaraderie I experienced. Although my term expired after three years, I made friends that will last a lifetime.

As with most boards, we were encouraged to get involved in committees. Since my background was in writing and marketing, I was asked to help develop the organization's marketing plan and chair the newly formed Marketing Committee. Our primary tasks included branding, website development, and the annual report. Secondary tasks included researching and writing the organization's mission, history, vision statement, success stories, marketing collateral, and a press kit. With the help of a graphic designer and two other talented board members, we tackled our assignments with great aplomb.

However, one strong, productive committee does not a successful board make. Our high-volume output couldn't rival the high-volume politics that dominated this organization. Here is a summary of the key issues that strangled this board and some recommended solutions.

Although the Chairman of the Board had held his position for 11 years and had earned the respect of officials in the parent organization, a few members of the board lobbied to enforce term limits and vote him out of office. Unbeknownst to the board or to the Chairman himself, supporters of a second rival candidate then took control of the Nominating Committee. The Chairman resigned under pressure. A third candidate was nominated from the floor and won the election. Supporters of the second candidate left the election disappointed, and the newly elected board chair was left to pick up the pieces.

This board would have benefited from mediation — early in the election process — to expose hidden agendas, to settle disputes caused by unclear bylaws and nominating procedures, and to resolve conflicts with disgruntled staff. In fact, mediation is the best tool to help in obtaining a resolution. Why? Because mediation is non-adversarial and helps solve problems more quickly.[5]

Case 1D: Unclear Mission

Even though the mission statement of this volunteer board appeared on its website and in other documents, board members were still unclear about their role on the board. Their role of overseeing funding was clear enough, but what were they supposed to do to "connect county residents to jobs," as their mission states? The reason board members were recruited in the first place was for their expertise in business, labor, education, government, and faith-based organizations. In order for these board members to understand their mission more clearly, they had to become more actively engaged in the process of "connecting county residents to jobs."

This board could have benefitted from brainstorming sessions on how their business or industry sector could help (or was helping) with job creation. They needed to identify best practices and ways to "connect county residents to jobs" as their mission states, or they will find it difficult to retain members, yet alone recruit new ones. The value of this organization and its mission (its "holy work") must become clear and obvious to everyone involved.

Do these issues sound familiar? If so, you need to address them sooner than later because unresolved conflicts will greatly diminish the success of your organization. A well-planned, well-executed conflict resolution program may prove to be one of the most important programs your organization ever implements. I have no doubt that it would have helped this talented board get back on track and refocused on its mission.

Case 1E: Disagreement over Mission and Vision

As a member of one board of directors, I volunteered to chair the Public Relations Committee, writing press releases and copy for the quarterly newsletter. Then, after serving four years on the board of directors, I was elected president of the organization. The term limit for this volunteer

---

5   "Mediation in the Nonprofit Organization," *Mediate.com*, 2014, <http://www.mediate.com/articles/henderson.cfm>.

position was two years, a limitation I gratefully appreciated and accepted; I was unanimously re-elected the second year.

What happened to the board after my two-year term is worth sharing with you, not only for the lessons it taught me, but also to demonstrate how important it is for every board member to understand the mission, vision, and history of the organization and what can happen if these are compromised in any way. But first, some background.

The idea of changing the name of this organization was first popularized by members of the board who believed the name represented the membership base more realistically and would help increase the reach of the organization and, consequently, membership. At first blush, this sounded like a good idea, but the board needed to gather data, research the ramifications, and do its homework before it could make an informed decision.

Unfortunately, in the board's zeal to implement the name change, homework flew out the window. Before a vote could be taken by the entire organization, before the bylaws could be amended to change the name, and even before legal counsel could be consulted, the name change announcement came out in the papers. The tumultuous conflict that ensued divided the organization, severed relationships, and prompted an exodus from the board of directors. In retrospect, I believe this conflict had two fundamental causes.

First, by changing the name of the organization, the board was also changing the organization's mission, vision, and geographical area as defined in its bylaws. Despite the lack of consensus on the board, the organization tried to change the name any way.

Second, this board needed to slow down, take more time to plan, reach consensus, and engage all stakeholders before implementing the name change, particularly since the change would have required changing the bylaws first. Per *Roberts Rules of Order Newly Revised,* Section 39 on improper motions: "Motions that conflict with the corporate charter, constitution or bylaws of a society, or with procedural rules prescribed by national, state, or local laws are out of order, and if any motion of this kind is adopted, it is null and void."[6] When put to a second vote, this board

---

[6]   Henry M. Robert et al. "Improper Motions," *Roberts Rules of Order Newly Revised,* 10th ed. (Cambridge, MA: Da Capo Press, 2000) 332, lines 15-18.

voted "no bylaw changes." Consequently, the name and geographical area were not changed. But by that time irreparable damage had been done.

Neighboring volunteer boards considered the name change a hostile takeover of their geographical area and a potential threat to their ability to attract and retain members by "causing confusion in the industry." Some officers, members, and past presidents (including me) objected to losing the community focus. Even worse, the general membership had not been consulted or involved in any discussions, so members were left wondering why the board wanted to change the organization's name in the first place.

Case 1F: Disregard for an Organization's History

By changing the organization's name, the board was perceived to be turning its back on its roots, dating back to the 1950s. Its founders had worked hard to shape its present identity, and the organization had earned a stellar reputation as a vital part of the community. Changing its name was perceived as a blatant disregard for its history, its identity, and its hard-earned reputation, which had taken over 50 years, thousands of members, and millions of membership dollars to accomplish.

This board could have benefited from a review of its long, community-focused history. How "vital" is your organization to the community you serve? What has it done to make itself "a vital part of that community"? The best board members will be those who can answer these questions. They will understand the organization's past, including when it was founded, who founded it, where it has been located, and why it has the name that it has.

In summary, every board needs a clear mission, purpose, vision, and history. No matter what type of organization it is, you need to keep these principles in mind:

- Your *mission statement* should explain your organization's reason for existence. It should describe who you are and what you do. Every Board member should know this mission.
- Your *vision statement* should describe what your organization intends to become or achieve for the long term, say ten years from now. Every board member should know this vision.
- Your *history* should provide dates, names, and key milestones that helped define your organization's purpose and helped shape its present identity. Every Board member should know this history.

If we can learn from our mistakes, then perhaps we won't make the same ones in the future. Or, in the words of philosopher George Santayana, "Those who cannot remember the past are condemned to repeat it."[7] We must not let the fear of making mistakes prevent us from seeking the best, most meaningful ways to serve as volunteers. Sister Gwendolyn's advice is worth repeating here: "A man's reach should exceed his grasp, or what's a heaven for?"

---

[7] "Santayana Quotations," *Indiana University School of Liberal Arts*, 2011, <http://iat.iupui.edu/santayana/content/santayana-quotations>.

CHAPTER 2

Org chart, bylaws, roles

"In the successful organization, no detail is too small to escape close attention."
--Lou Holtz

Lesson 2: Every Board needs an org chart, bylaws, and clear statement of roles and responsibilities

Once you have determined the organization's mission and values, ask to see its org chart, bylaws, and statement of roles and responsibilities. If the board has none of these, I repeat: abandon all hope for this organization. If it has all of these, then find out if the bylaws are outdated, being followed, or being ignored. Some critical questions to ask: (1) What are the roles and responsibilities of officers, standing committees, and staff? (2) Who appoints the committee chairs, and how do board members get on these committees? (3) To whom do the Executive Administrator and staff report? (4) How much do they get paid, and who reviews their performance? (5) Is the board really the decision-making body? (6) Or does the board just rubberstamp the decisions of the Executive Administrator and staff? Find out how work gets done. If you cannot get a straight answer (or don't like what you hear), find another place to volunteer. You won't be sorry.

Case 2A: Same Officers Elected Year after Year

In the 60s I belonged to a county-sponsored volunteer organization in the city of Bismarck, North Dakota. What was different about this organization was that it met in an urban, not rural setting. Nevertheless, the goal was the same — to have parents teach important life skills, such as cooking, sewing, woodworking, time management, record keeping, public speaking, and more. In the 90s, when I had children of my own, I started a similar club in New Jersey. I persuaded my husband to be co-leader, explaining that together we could teach our two children and their friends some of the same things our parents taught us. Seeing the value in this family-centered activity, he willingly agreed.

Our first group had only five members: our two children and the three Japanese children who lived next door. The first year we taught basic sewing techniques (e.g., how to thread a needle and sew on buttons); the following year we tackled basic cooking. Although our original members are now in their twenties, my husband and I have remained active in the organization. Why? Because we believe in family-focused activities and, as parents, we believe in teaching and learning right alongside the children. We also understand that the problems inherent in this volunteer organization could exist anywhere. For example. . .

The same people have been calling the shots on the board for decades. Fortunately, they are knowledgeable and demonstrate good judgment. One of them provides invaluable history and insight for the board. Unfortunately, they see no reason to retire or change anything about the organization. So year after year, the same people on the board vote themselves into office — without term limits. I served as Vice President for a few months, but my efforts to revitalize the organization with goal-directed mini-workshops for leaders met with considerable resistance. Like many boards, this one had become entrenched and unyielding.

This board could have benefitted from a process workshop to improve communication and increase participation. The primary goal of this type of workshop should be to encourage a democratic, free flow of ideas. The secondary goal should be to define roles and responsibilities. Additionally, this organization needed to limit board members to two consecutive terms. Many organizations stagger terms of service so that one half or one third of the board is elected every one or two years for terms of two to four years. By staggering terms of service, the board profits from the experience of veteran board members while gaining the fresh perspective of new board members.

Case 2B: No Staff Continuity

To complicate matters further, this volunteer board didn't have a full-time Executive Administrator due to budget cuts. Instead, it employed a series of part-time staff to manage the organization's many activities, resulting in frequent staff turnover. The lack of continuity of leadership continues to plague the organization.

This board needs to examine the pay structure of its administration and staff and, most importantly, the reasons why they are constantly leaving. Doing nothing will not solve the turnover problem. In addition, this board needs to recruit, retain, and reward an Executive Administrator who demonstrates loyalty, commitment, creativity, and respect for this honorable organization and its volunteers. Finally, increasing the number of committed parent volunteers who provide leadership and continuity to the organization will be key to its survival.

Case 2C: Unclear Organizational Structure

I have been very fortunate to have had great mentors along the way. When I was President of my Alumni Association, it was the Alumni Director, Sister Gwendolyn. When I was President of another board, my mentor was the outgoing President. Like Sister Gwendolyn, this gentleman was gifted with excellent organizational and interpersonal skills. When his two-year term had expired and he passed the presidential torch to me, he explained that although the organizational structure he developed was working, we still needed to clarify the roles and responsibilities of each committee and think about ways to add value to the organization. I welcomed the challenge.

I began by developing an *organizational chart* (aka org chart) showing the inter-relationships between the board of directors, Executive Administrator, and the committees. The org chart helped me define reporting structures, lines of authority, and responsibilities. The org chart in **Figure 1** is an example of what I mean.

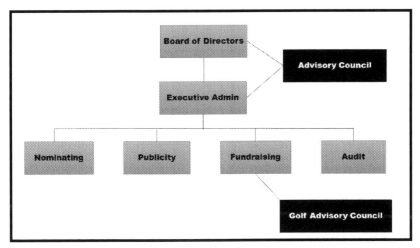

Figure 1. Sample Organizational Structure for a Board of Directors

I firmly believe that every volunteer board should have an org chart outlining its management team. Without one, people will be unsure of who they report to and what their jobs are. And, if people are unsure of what's required of them, errors and omissions can occur, creating tension, miscommunication, and inefficiencies that cost time and money.[8]

Equally important, every volunteer board should have bylaws that are up to date. Are your organization's bylaws outdated, being followed, or simply being ignored? I had inherited bylaws that were outdated and not being followed. Fortunately, we had two committed volunteers willing to take on the task of bylaw revision with me: a long-standing board member, plus a talented lawyer who championed this pro bono effort. Once the revisions were drafted, special meetings of the board were required to vote on each section of the document, and because the bylaws hadn't been revised for some time, the effort was quite time consuming. However, the finished document was well worth the time and effort and proved invaluable in clarifying roles and responsibilities. I learned early on, though, that the bylaws weren't the only issue plaguing this volunteer organization.

---

[8]   "Managing People," *SmallBizConnect*, n. d., <http://toolkit.smallbiz.nsw.gov.au/part/4/17/79>.

Case 2D: Unreliable Committee Chairs

Although this volunteer board had made great strides with organizational restructuring and bylaws during my term, we still had miles to go to get board members to *perform* their roles and responsibilities. One committee chair, uncertain of his committee's purpose, simply held monthly brainstorming sessions with his volunteers. After several months of meetings and no action plan, his committee membership dwindled. Another committee chair simply held no meetings at all. Again, the volunteers started to drift away.

Early intervention is critical when committee chairs are struggling to get things done. I discussed the situation with the former President, and we agreed that I would speak privately with both leaders and discuss our strategy to "save" these committees. I would let these two committee chairs keep their titles until their one-year term was up, but in the meantime, I would appoint a co-chair for each committee to help create agendas, engage volunteers, and report to me and the board. This solution was effective because it saved the leader face, kept the remaining volunteers on the team, and gave the new co-chairs valuable experience in case they wanted to become chair at the end of the term.

Case 2E: Unclear Role of the Executive Administrator

Every board of directors should be responsible for financial oversight, management oversight, legal oversight, and program oversight. In addition, boards often hire an Executive Administrator to execute policies, programs, and initiatives. This person is often more involved than the board of directors in the day-to-day operations of the organization. As with most boards, this volunteer board struggled to define the role of the Executive Administrator. Since every decision the board made relating to budget and compensation affected the Executive Administrator, the Executive Administrator would be voting on her own salary, a potential conflict of interest.[9]

---

[9] Mollie Cullinane, "Nonprofit Law Basics: Can the Executive Director Serve on the Board of Directors?" *Cullinane Law Group,* 16 April 2012, <http://www.cullinanelaw.com/nonprofit-law-basics-can-the-executive-director-serve-on-the-board-of-directors/>.

To handle this potential conflict, we took the following steps:

- We invited the Executive Administrator to attend board meetings as a guest instead of as a voting member.
- We excluded the Executive Administrator from board discussions involving compensation.
- We developed performance review policies and procedures and assigned the Executive Administrator's performance review to the President and Governance Committee, who evaluated work performance and recommended compensation to the Board.
- We added this section to our bylaws to help clarify the role of the Executive Administrator:

<u>Section 2</u>: Executive Administrator

The Board of Directors shall employ an Executive Administrator and shall fix the salary and other considerations of the Executive Administrator's employment.

The Executive Administrator:

1. May serve as the corporate secretary of the organization;
2. Shall be the chief administrative officer of the organization and report directly to the President;
3. Shall serve as administrator to the Board of Directors and see to the preparation of notices, agenda, and minutes of meetings of the board;
4. Shall serve as an advisor to the President;
5. Shall assemble information and data, and prepare special reports;
6. Shall be the liaison between the President and all committees;
7. Shall act as facilitator for all committees;
8. Shall be responsible for the administration of all programs in accordance with the policies and regulations of the Board of Directors;
9. Shall be responsible for directing and supervising all employees;

10. Shall contribute actively to the preparation of an operating budget, in cooperation with the Executive Committee, covering all activities of the organization;

11. Shall perform such other tasks as may be requested reasonably, from time to time, by the President.

Employment as Executive Administrator does not confer membership status, or the rights and privileges of membership, upon the Executive Administrator.

Whatever your Board decides the Executive Administrator's status should be, keep in mind that his/her insights into the daily operations of the organization are essential for the board to make informed decisions.

Case 2F: Outdated, Insufficient Information for Board Members

During my three-year term on another volunteer board, I discovered that most board members were unaware that an org chart existed for the organization and that there was a handbook for members, outlining our roles and responsibilities. In truth, most of us never had any orientation or training. So I was surprised (and quite pleased) when the parent organization issued a five-page description of our "roles and responsibilities." This updated document outlined very clearly the responsibilities of the Chairman, the Executive Administrator, and the entire board. However, it was never used as a training tool for the board. Neither had the board's bylaws been updated, reviewed by, or clearly explained to us. Without these key documents, we were quite unclear about our roles and responsibilities — a common issue with volunteer boards.

Board members cannot make well-informed decisions or oversee an organization effectively with outdated, insufficient information. In the three years I served on this volunteer board, I never received training of any kind. If your Executive Administrator hasn't developed an orientation session (or at least an orientation binder) for your board, it should be a priority as soon as possible. At the very least, a board member's orientation binder should include up-to-date information on the following essentials: your mission statement, vision statement, bylaws, org chart, and statement of roles and responsibilities. Just distributing this information to board members isn't enough; the documents need to be discussed regularly and often. Even the best, most committed board members may not take the time or be motivated to read the information.

The Executive Administrator (or a designated trainer) should be responsible for the continuous, ongoing training of board members. This training should be part of a comprehensive strategic plan that has been developed in conjunction with the board and supplemented by regular progress reports. Ultimately, this will help keep the board's sights focused on the long-term goals and the mission of the organization. Also, regular reports based on this plan will help keep board members apprised of progress toward organizational goals and provide part of the basis for evaluation of the Executive Administrator. **Figure 2** provides a sample agenda for an orientation session for a board of directors.[10]

Sample Agenda: Board of Directors Orientation

- Welcome and review of agenda
- Introduction of participants
- Overview of organization: mission, vision, history, etc.
- Orientation to board manual: Articles of Incorporation, bylaws, etc.
- Board structure & roles and responsibilities
- Overview of board operations
- Review of strategic plan
- Administrative activities
- Next steps and meeting evaluation

Figure 2. Orientation Session for Board Members

---

[10] "Training Module 5: Part B, The Board of Directors – Recruitment, Training & Effectiveness," *Southern Early Childhood Association,* n. d, 13, <http://www.google.com/url?sa=t&rct=j&q=&esrc=s&source=web&cd=1&ved =0CB8QFjAA&url=http%3A%2F%2Fwww.southernearlychildhood.org%2 Fupload%2Fpdf%2FTraining%2520Module%25205%2520Part%2520B-Board%2520of%2520Directors-Training%2520Recruitment%2520%2520 Effectiveness.ppt&ei=Ggq_U9DXLZahyATEmYKYDg&usg=AFQjCNG0fsb h75ofQKVEN6ahtKRED1zNZw&bvm=bv.70810081,d.aWw>.

Case 2G: Failure to Focus on Larger Issues or Consensus Building

Even the best volunteers have limited tolerance for ambiguity, especially when it comes to their roles and responsibilities. To attract and retain board members, your organization must not look confused, divided, or disorganized. You must be able to tell people exactly what their responsibilities are and point them to the documents that spell out these responsibilities. More importantly, your board meetings cannot be so concerned with minutiae (trivial details) that you fail to focus on larger issues, such as your mission and long-term goals.

Like many boards, this one could have benefitted from focusing more closely on matters needing board oversight as well as more succinct reports from officers, staff, and committee chairs. Otherwise, volunteers are likely to feel their time is being wasted, or worse, serving on this board is itself a waste of time. Before introducing a topic on the agenda or asking board members to vote on an issue, for example, the Chairman could explain where in the bylaws, handbook, or other documentation, it says board members have this responsibility. Not only will board members appreciate this information, but explanations like this will also help them better understand their role in the organization and provide a context for the issue at hand. With this information, board members are more likely to become engaged in a dialogue that leads to consensus-building. I'm reminded of the advice Sister Hugo once gave me when I was a doing my student teaching in her classroom: "Never miss an opportunity to teach something." Any Executive Administrator or Chairman of the Board could benefit from this advice.

Case 2H: Confusion over Who Appoints Committee Chairs

The work of every volunteer committee should be directed by the board, and the board should vote on and approve all committee chairs. Why? Because without board approval, chair appointments can easily fall victim to favoritism or the personal bias of the individual making the appointment. Confusion over who appoints committee chairs became an issue on this volunteer board when we learned that the Executive Administrator had recruited and appointed chairs for several committees (e.g., Bylaws Committee, Nominating Committee, and others) without approval/vote by the board. This problem raised a critical question: Who has the authority to appoint committee chairs? After considerable research, we found the answer in the organization's statement of roles and responsibilities: *"The Chairman of the Board appoints the chairs of all councils and committees."* Despite reprimands from the Chairman and protests from the Executive Committee, the Executive Administrator persisted in recruiting volunteers to chair committees, elevating them even to Executive Committee status! Imagine the Chairman's surprise when these newly appointed committee chairs suddenly appeared at Executive Committee meetings. The conflict that ensued caused considerable damage to the organization.

If your organization doesn't already have a policy for appointing committee chairs, you need to create one and include it in your bylaws. For example: "The President shall, with the advice and counsel of the Sr. Vice President, subject to approval by the Board of Directors, establish all committees, appoint Vice Presidents to chair the committees, and assist in the selection of committee personnel." *Robert's Rules of Order* emphasizes that there is one committee chair the president may not appoint, the Nominating Committee:

> The nominating committee should be elected by the organization, wherever possible, or else by the executive board. Although in organizing new society it may be feasible for the chair to appoint the nominating committee, in an organized society, *the president should not appoint this committee or be a member of it* — ex officio or otherwise. The bylaws may provide that 'the President shall appoint all committees except the Nominating Committee.'[11]

If you're following *Robert's Rules,* then your president shouldn't be on your Nominating Committee and, more importantly, should be excluded from serving on it. This requirement protects both the president and the committee from accusations of self-perpetuation and favoritism. However, this exclusion doesn't mean the committee is prohibited from consulting with the president for his/her advice or opinion.

In short, committee chairs need to be carefully *screened and appointed by the board,* and committee members need to know their roles and responsibilities. The best way to convey this information is to develop a "charter" for the committee. The charter should spell out who appoints the

---

[11]   Robert 419, lines 7-13.

committee chair, the committee's purpose, relationship to the governing body, composition, terms of service, officers and how elected, meeting frequency, and reporting obligations. Optimally, the charter should explain how the work of this committee relates to the overall strategic plan of the organization. **Figure 3** shows a sample committee charter.[12]

[12] Adapted from "Sample Advisory Committee Charter: Charter for Agricultural Advisory Committee," *Program Planning Handbook* (Colombia, MO: University of Missouri, n. d.) 97.13

<http://www.google.com/url?sa=t&rct=j&q=&esrc=s&source=web&cd=1&ved=0CB8QFjAA&url=http%3A%2F%2Fdass.missouri.edu%2Faged%2Fresources%2Fhandbook%2Fchap2%2F02AdvisoryCharter.doc&ei=V_XkU_mTItWBygTr1oCoBg&usg=AFQjCNEA0Uj74y_Zs6T3UKYf8AhlB9kZog&bvm=bv.72676100,d.aWw>.

Sample Committee Charter

I.   The Committee will be called the [name of committee].

It is authorized by the [name of governing body] and will serve at the pleasure of the governing body. The President shall, subject to approval by the Board of Directors, appoint the chair of this Committee and assist in the selection of committee personnel.

II.   Purpose

The Committee is created for the purpose of [statement of purpose] and shall limit its activities to advising on matters that directly concern [name of committee]. The specific purposes of the Committee may include the following responsibilities: [list them here]

III.   Relationship of Committee to the Governing Body

It is the role and sole prerogative of the Board to enact policy. The [name of committee] is expected to offer recommendations for [fill in the blank] and to provide information relevant to policy about [fill in the blank].

IV.   Membership

Composition: The [name of committee] shall consist of [number of] members. Members will be selected and appointed by the Board. Committee members must be [state member qualifications here, if any].

Term: A term of membership shall last for three years, with one-third of the membership appointed each year. Terms shall not be renewable within 11 months after conclusion of an earlier term. Terms will begin on August 1.

V.   Organizational Structure

Officers: The committee will have a chair, vice chair, and recording secretary who are elected for one-year terms by committee members. Elections will be held at the first meeting of the new membership year.

VI. Procedural Rules

Meetings: The committee will meet at least [number of] times per year. Written notices of upcoming meetings will be mailed to members at least ten days before a meeting.

Minutes: Minutes of each meeting will be kept. Copies will be mailed to the board and committee membership within two weeks after a meeting.

Recommendations and Reports: Committee recommendations and reports will be submitted in writing to the board. Documents will include both suggested action and justification for suggestions. The board will respond to such recommendations in writing.

Dismissal: Members who are absent without reasonable cause from three successive meetings will be considered to have resigned their seat. The committee will move to fill the position.

Public Announcements: Committee members shall not report opinions expressed in meetings, nor shall they report independently on committee action.

Figure 3. Sample Committee Charter

In summary, a volunteer board cannot function effectively without a solid organizational structure, up-to-date bylaws, or clear statement of roles and responsibilities. Not having these documents in place can lead to serious conflicts. Every volunteer board would be well-served by implementing the following:

- A process workshop to improve communication skills and encourage a democratic, free flow of ideas.
- A definition of term limits for all board members.
- A well-written statement of the roles and responsibilities of all board members, as well as for the Executive Administrator, as part of its bylaws.
- A procedure for replacing unreliable committee chairs.

- An orientation session for new board members with periodic updates to keep all board members apprised of new programs, policies, and procedures.
- A clearly written policy for the appointment of committee chairs.
- Succinct meeting agendas and committee reports that reiterate how the work of the officers and committees relate to the overall strategic plan of the organization.
- A charter for every committee, one that clearly explains the purpose of the committee, its relationship to the governing body, reporting obligations, and more.

As Lou Holz has so wisely said, "In the successful organization, no detail is too small to escape close attention."

CHAPTER 3

Leadership

"Servant-leadership is all about making the goals clear and then rolling your sleeves up and doing whatever it takes to help people win. In that situation, they don't work for you, you work for them."

--Ken Blanchard

Lesson 3: Every Board needs effective leadership

No organization can function with a Board Chair who is a "Godzilla," or conversely, a "Casper Milk Toast." In the first case, the lack of tolerance for DIFFERENT points of view will destroy all trust and camaraderie. In the second case, tolerance for EVERY point of view, though helpful for communication, can bring decision making to a screeching halt. Both intolerance and indecision are toxic for volunteer boards. To be effective, the Board Chair must be a mentor, not a tyrant or an indecisive leader, relying solely on the input of a few "inbred" friends to agree with what the Chair says. An effective Board Chair must be a respected peer — a team player who encourages different points of view, one who doesn't micromanage, delegates authority, and trusts that others will follow through. A strong team on the Executive Committee — empowered by the Board — can keep the power of the Chair in check or can get an indecisive Chair to act. An effective Executive Committee can also provide "the bench" or succession plan for future leaders. To help ensure continuity of leadership, the next Board Chair should be mentored by the current Chair and serve on the Executive Committee. Succession planning helps ensure that experienced and capable individuals will be prepared for leadership roles and responsibilities as they become available.

Case 3A: Demonstrating Servant Leadership

My first experience as President of a volunteer board was strongly influenced by the low-ego approach of the Benedictine nuns, the sponsoring body of my alma mater, the University of Mary in Bismarck, North Dakota. Sister Gwendolyn, the university's first Alumni Director, was a wonderful mentor and example of a servant leader, one who made the organization's goals clear and then rolled up her sleeves alongside her volunteers to help accomplish them. Under her tutelage, I learned to appreciate the importance of goal setting and then making the organization's goals clear to everyone involved: in newsletters, at events, through publications, whenever the opportunity presented itself.

Furthermore, I learned that people will not follow a leader until he/she shows genuine interest in THEM. How did Sister Gwendolyn do this? First, she was masterful at remembering details about a person. She took time to get to know her volunteers as individuals — as valued human beings with unique gifts, families, and stories worth remembering! Second, she met with us via regular, informal interactions outside of board meetings: spontaneous lunches, chats over a cup of coffee, even invitations to join the nuns at evening prayer and Sunday liturgy. As Board members, we clearly enjoyed these interactions, evidenced by high levels of participation and attendance at meetings, open debate and questioning, and an atmosphere of mutual trust and respect. Third, and most important, Sister Gwendolyn had a knack for recruiting people who had a passion for the university's mission! Finally, whether she knew it or not, Sister Gwendolyn was creating a healthy organization, based on the six servant-leadership principles,[13] as shown in **Figure 4**.

---

[13] Jim Laub, "Servant Leadership: Defining Servant Leadership and the Healthy Organization," *OLAgroup*, 2014, <http://www.olagroup.com/Display.asp?Page=servant leadership>. Jim Laub holds a Doctorate in Educational Leadership and Adult Education from Florida Atlantic University. His dissertation and ongoing research have focused on the critical topic of servant leadership and organizational health.

Figure 4. Six Key Areas of a Healthy Organization

Valuing people, developing people, building community, displaying authenticity, providing leadership, and sharing leadership are the six key areas of a healthy organization, as posited by Dr. Jim Laub, Dean of the MacArthur School of Leadership at Palm Beach Atlantic University. These principles were practiced in Sister Gwendolyn's Alumni Association, cultivated in her Benedictine community, and exemplified in her style of leadership. Laub's definitions further explain her servant-style of leadership:

> **Servant Leadership** is an understanding and practice of leadership that places the good of those led over the self-interest of the leader. Servant leadership promotes the valuing and development of people, the building of community, the practice of authenticity, the providing of leadership for the good of those led and the sharing of power and status for the common good of each individual, the total organization and those served by the organization.[14]

---

[14] Laub.

The **Healthy Organization** is an organization in which the characteristics of servant leadership are displayed through the organizational culture and are valued and practiced by the leadership and workforce. This is a healthy, servant organization. One that puts the needs of others first and through that gains incredible strength and power throughout the organization.[15]

The power and strength of Sister Gwendolyn's Alumni Association came from "putting the needs of others first" and from aligning people, programs, and events with our mission. If your board is falling apart (or is in danger of doing so), examine how well you are applying the six principles outlined above. When one or more of the six areas is missing, the health of the organization will be seriously jeopardized. Here are some examples to illustrate my point.

Case 3B: Sharing Power and Status

One of the first things I did as President of a volunteer board was to meet individually with every officer and committee chair, as Sister Gwendolyn had done with me, to listen to them and formulate our collective goals for the coming year. At the end of each meeting, I typed up these notes (evidence that I had really listened and valued their comments) and then worked with each individual to summarize his/her goals in two succinct words. Why two words? Because I wanted each officer and committee chair to present his/her goals to the full membership at the upcoming annual meeting. Projecting two words on a slide behind each presenter helped the speaker keep his/her comments focused and brief. It worked. The result was an engaging presentation of our goals for the coming year and a succinct presentation of our collective vision. Sharing the podium with my peers and letting THEM explain our vision also demonstrated that I trusted them and valued their skills, abilities, input, and service to the organization. I think even Sister Gwendolyn would have been pleased with the clarity and passion demonstrated by these wonderful volunteers.

---

[15] Laub.

Case 3C: Not Valuing People

Whenever the administration changes in an organization, you can expect changes throughout the organization. New leaders often what to put their "stamp" on the organization. In the case of this volunteer board, the new President chose to put her stamp on the annual meeting. Although each officer was invited to address the full membership, the President did not spend time working individually with them beforehand to focus their presentations. Slide presentations and individual goal statements were cut. The image she portrayed at the annual meeting was of a new leader, reluctant to share the spotlight. The message she portrayed (consciously or unconsciously) was that whatever she had to say was of greater value than her peers.

This President needed to trust her peers, listen more attentively to them, and share the spotlight. She could have shown she valued people more by taking the time to help them formulate their goals and shape their presentations. At Board meetings, her inflexibility and "Godzilla" style of leadership were further evidenced by her refusal to listen to opposing views, cutting people off with statements such as, "there is no discussion." By dismissing people like this, she left them feeling that neither they nor their comments had much value. Eventually, the lack of tolerance for different points of view destroyed trust and camaraderie on the board, and she resigned after a single term.

Case 3D: Not Developing People

Unlike Sister Gwendolyn, the President of this volunteer board didn't see mistakes as opportunities to learn and grow, nor did she accept the responsibility of helping people develop their full potential. Her style was simply to TELL others what to do, instead of working alongside them to SHOW them how.

Growth and development must be encouraged in a healthy organization. To help develop her people, this President needed to spend more time getting to know their individual talents, affirming them as people. She needed to recognize their creativity and accomplishments — especially the time they so generously donated — and then celebrate their successes. In short, she needed to build them up and affirm their efforts. Without affirming them, this President missed a powerful opportunity to win their trust, support, and admiration. No organization will follow a leader who simply tells them what to do.

Case 3E: Not Sharing Leadership

This President found it difficult to share leadership. For example, she never consulted the Sr. Vice President on any matters, even though the bylaws required his advice and counsel: "The President shall, *with the advice and counsel of the Sr. Vice President*, subject to approval of the Board of Directors, establish all committees, appoint Vice Presidents to chair the committees, and assist in the selection of committee personnel." Her refusal to share leadership with the Sr. Vice President resulted in numerous spiteful actions towards him; namely, she removed him from several committees, she cancelled two of his sub-committees, and worse, she wasn't transparent in revealing these actions to the board, leading them to think that "all was well." Not communicating openly, proactively, and transparently with her Sr. Vice President and members of the board was an abuse of power — an obvious indication of an unhealthy organization.

Healthy organizations recognize that every leader has power and must continually make choices about how to use it. This President needed to share her power with others so that others could lead. Sharing leadership would have allowed her people, in particular her Sr. Vice President, to become engaged in making decisions and developing a collective vision. It would have empowered others by affirming their status and inherent value. In a healthy organization, every member needs to be valued and acknowledged for individual contributions. If your volunteer board has a President who is reluctant to share leadership, you have an unhealthy organization.

Case 3F: Building Relationships Takes Time

During my three-year term on another volunteer board, I had the pleasure of working with another excellent mentor, one who had served as Chairman of the Board for 11 years. What I admired most about him was his authenticity, humility, and servant style of leadership. He proactively sought to build professional relationships with his management team, frequently engaging us in conversations outside of board meetings about our backgrounds, preferences, and capabilities. He understood that building relationships takes time, and he willing donated hundreds of hours leading this organization, plus several other non-profit organizations in the region.

As a servant-leader, he took great care to engage the Executive Committee in all aspects of governance and didn't try to micromanage us. He took an active role in succession planning and in developing strategy, but he didn't assume "supreme" authority over us. Rather, he delegated responsibilities to his management team and then trusted us to follow through. His low-ego style of management kept the organization ticking for 11 years, until a dissenting faction of opponents pressured him to resign. The following unfortunate situations illustrate how even effective leaders can be ousted by board members who do not share the leader's vision.

Case 3G: Not Displaying Authenticity

In healthy organizations, leaders must be open, real, approachable and accountable to others. The Chairman of this volunteer board had these qualities; he never suggested that he was higher than others because of his position. The Executive Administrator, on the other hand, found it difficult to be accountable to others. She seemed reluctant to learn from her mistakes, from poor performance reviews, or even from the Chairman's admonitions. She frequently took credit for the work of others. She seemed to need to protect her position at all cost, sacrificing authenticity in the process. The result? We could not trust what she had to say.

This board could have terminated the Executive Administrator, based on her lack of integrity, lack of authenticity, and poor performance reviews. However, neither the Chairman of the Board nor the parent organization had the will to terminate her, nor did they try to seek professional mediation to "mend fences." Volunteers do not thrive in negative situations like this. When terms were up, a flurry of resignations ensued, including the Chairman's, forcing the board to hold a special election.

In healthy organizations, the leaders willingly accept their roles and responsibilities; in this one, the Executive Administrator could not. She refused to accept the authority of the Chairman, whom the parent organization deemed the "spokesperson" for the organization. Rather, she believed she was the spokesperson and was not accountable to the Chairman or to the Executive Committee. Her personal ambition was diametrically opposed to the servant-style leadership of the Chairman.

When this happens, relationships break down and boards fall apart. Restoring them can be impossible, and the solutions are limited.

Case 3H: Not Providing Leadership

Any board that has had to work with an underperforming Executive Administrator will recognize the necessity of investing time and effort in contingency planning to determine who will be responsible for helping the Executive Administrator improve if there are problems, and what appropriate remedial actions will be taken. On this board, although the Chairman of the Board and the Vice Chair had developed a plan for remediation, the Executive Administrator refused to comply. Instead, she lobbied other board members to come to her defense. The problem was exacerbated by the fact that most board members were unaware that there was any problem with the Executive Administrator's performance reviews or behavior, believing "all was well."

Thomas Jefferson once said that "honesty is the first chapter in the book of wisdom." The leaders of this organization should have maintained a strict "no surprises" policy with the board, including honest, clear, and open communication. They could have provided better leadership by telling the board about the situation instead of keeping silent. They could have encouraged accountability to the goals set for themselves and others. In short, they could have taken the initiative and been fully transparent with everyone on the board. Instead, the officers resigned, the situation was never resolved, and the performance of the Executive Administrator was never questioned. They left. She stayed. She won.

Case 3I: Not Building Community

According to Dr. Laub, "Healthy organizations have a different way of looking at how people work together. They desire to build community; a sense that all are part of a loving, caring team with a compelling shared vision to accomplish."[16] This board did not take time to build relationships or get to know one another. Board members contributed primarily as "lone rangers" rather than teams. Instead of working collaboratively, there were mostly committees of "one." Committee recruitment wasn't a priority,

---

[16] Laub.

nor were there open lines of communication with other stakeholders. In short, this organization was reluctant to build community or to serve one another. Eventually board factions developed — another obvious sign of an unhealthy organization.

To avoid the development of board factions, the Chairman of the Board needed to work harder at team building with the entire board, not just his executive team. How? First, by personally recruiting people for committees. Second, by taking time to get to know everyone on the board, showing his personal interest in THEM. Team building and community building go hand in hand. This board needed to experience the benefits of collaboration, teamwork, and building community. It needed to become a healthy organization, "One that puts the needs of others first and through that gains incredible strength and power throughout the organization."[17]

In summary, servant leadership is an understanding and practice of leadership that places the good of those led over the self-interest of the leader. I firmly believe that when a volunteer board has a servant-leader at the helm, it is more likely to thrive. Why? Because servant leaders understand and appreciate these six key principles:

- the valuing of people
- the development of people
- the building of community
- the practice of authenticity
- the providing of leadership for the good of those led
- the sharing of power and status for the common good of each individual, the total organization, and those served by the organization.

Effective leaders must be flexible and must adapt themselves according to the situation. The Board Chair must be a team player who encourages different points of view, doesn't micromanage, delegates authority, and trusts that others will follow through. If the leader of your volunteer board simply tells people what to do, doesn't value or trust them, doesn't share leadership, isn't fully transparent with the board, takes credit for others' work, refuses to be accountable for poor performance, and doesn't try to build community, you have an unhealthy volunteer organization.

---

[17] Laub.

CHAPTER 4

Moral Courage

"I prefer to be true to myself, even at the hazard of incurring the ridicule of others, rather than to be false, and to incur my own abhorrence."

-- Frederick Douglass

Lesson 4: Board members must demonstrate moral courage

The individuals who serve on volunteer boards are seldom engaged in the day-day-operations of the organization, nor do they want to be. These responsibilities are usually assigned to the Executive Administrator who may or may not wield a giant stick! I have served on boards that were quite content with this arrangement because board members really weren't interested in doing any "heavy lifting" for the organization, preferring instead to follow the leader, like sheep, and avoid conflict. This "see no evil, hear no evil, speak no evil" behavior can have devastating consequences. If key responsibilities are controlled by the Executive Administrator, there can be no balance of power. I have witnessed entire boards controlled by Executive Administrators who have ignored unethical behavior, rejected transparency, and even misused funds. And board members, out of fear or indifference, did nothing! To be effective, a volunteer board must have moral courage — the courage to take action for moral reasons despite the adverse consequences. The best volunteer boards are those whose members aren't afraid to speak up and, when presented with unethical behavior, have the moral courage to take action. Moral courage is what's needed when pressures in your organization or workplace threaten to compromise your values and principles.

As individuals, we may not be able to pinpoint exactly HOW our individual values and ethics were formed, but I believe we can identify WHO and WHAT helped shape them. I know that growing up in a devout and loving Catholic family and educated by devout and loving Benedictine nuns definitely shaped my values. In fact, the mission of my alma mater, the University of Mary, clearly states the importance of moral courage as a key value in educating students: "Founded to prepare leaders in the service of truth, the University of Mary is distinctive in our education and formation of servant leaders with **moral courage**, global understanding, and commitment to the common good."[18]

Sister Thomas Welder, President Emerita — one of my teachers, a former colleague, a mentor, and friend — further articulates the university's mission:

> Servant Leadership at the University of Mary is a pattern of living marked by competence in one's chosen profession, courage in making ethical decisions based on Benedictine values, and compassion in serving the needs of others. In a context of relationship to God, to one another, and to self, we believe that leadership is making a difference for good. Rooted in the Gospel and in the founding vision of the Benedictine Sisters to serve spiritual, intellectual, and cultural needs of others, the model for servant leadership is Jesus Himself. At the University of Mary students grow into leadership through service. Learners become leaders in the service of truth.[19]

As board members, we must have the courage to make ethical decisions and "become leaders in the service of truth," as Sister Thomas puts it. In fact, a powerful indication of a healthy board is its ability to seek the truth in the face of unethical or destructive situations. If the majority of board members don't agree that the behavior is unethical or destructive, there can be devastating consequences. Here are some of the experiences I have had with volunteer boards that presented opportunities for exercising moral courage.

---

[18] "About U-Mary: Our Statement of Mission & Identity," *University of Mary*, n. d., <http://www.umary.edu/about/mission/missionidentity.php>.

[19] "Our Mission: Servant Leadership at U-Mary," *University of Mary*, n. d., <http://www.umary.edu/about/mission/servantleadership.php>.

Case 4A: Dealing with Deception

In the 1980s, I was an associate professor of English at a community college. One of my administrative duties was to launch a "Writing across the Curriculum" program, aimed at helping faculty incorporate writing into their courses as an intrinsic way to help students LEARN the material, not just to TEST the material. To begin, my department head helped me recruit a board of senior faculty, including several department chairs, whom the College President proudly called his "College Writing Council." This enthusiastic advisory board met regularly to define our mission and identify the assumptions on which the program would be based. We unanimously agreed that our Writing across the Curriculum program would be based on the seven assumptions, as outlined in **Table 1.**

Table 1. Assumptions Developed by Advisory Board

No.	Assumption
1	The job of improving students' writing is simply too complex, too time-consuming to be undertaken by any one course or any one discipline.
2	The act of writing can be a means whereby students can master the content of almost any course.
3	Teaching writing is not simply a matter of correcting spelling, improving syntax, or stamping out mistakes in usage, but rather the teaching of basic processes students will need to use in discovering what they wish to say.
4	Frequent short writing assignments can be effective means of engaging students in and helping them examine these processes.
5	Various writing assignments make various intellectual demands upon the writer — demands which, if identified and taught one at a time, can provide sound and effective strategies for writing.
6	An understanding of audience and purpose is basic to all types of discourse and, therefore, is basic to discourse in the disciplines as well.
7	If we make complete assignments that help students to understand the nature of the task, we clarify the criteria for ourselves as well as the students.

As chairperson of this advisory board, I worked one-on-one with each member and with a number of other faculty volunteers to introduce them to our goals and get their buy in. To do this, I spent hours listening to them describe their courses, reviewing course objectives, identifying topics that would lend themselves to writing, and then helping them design purposeful writing activities. After six years of intensive effort, dozens of faculty meetings, and a comprehensive proposal and budget, we finally got the green light from the Faculty Senate and the College President for the first college-wide program, set to launch on June 5, 1987 with a faculty training workshop, for which each attendee was promised a small stipend.

On the day of the workshop, I arrived with materials, audio-visual equipment, and folders for each of the 15 faculty participants, including research and articles relevant to each person's discipline —from accounting to nursing, from business to computer science. But to my surprise, before I could begin, an Assistant Dean arrived and announced, "This workshop has been cancelled and the faculty will not be paid." She gave no explanation as to why the workshop had been cancelled. She simply made the announcement and left. We surmised that whatever funding had been allocated for Writing across the Curriculum had already been spent. Soon thereafter the administration changed hands, and no explanation was ever given. This lack of communication never resolved the feelings of deception and betrayal caused by broken promises to this dedicated group of faculty. I believe the situation could have been diffused (and even resolved) if the administration had simply been honest with the faculty.

Case 4B: Dealing with Conflicting Values

According to noted author and ethicist Michael Josephson, "Those who mobilize, direct, and motivate volunteers must be committed to the following core ethical values:[20]

1. Trustworthiness
2. Respect
3. Responsibility
4. Fairness
5. Caring
6. Citizenship

---

[20] Michael Josephson, *Making Ethical Decisions* (Los Angeles, CA: The Josephson Institute of Ethics, 2002) 7-14.

During my two-year term as President of one volunteer board, I was confronted with several situations that required ethical decisions. These are some of the lessons I learned, lessons related to all six of the ethical values listed above.

Case 4C: Lack of Trustworthiness (pillar #1)

Soon after my election as President of this volunteer board, I received a phone call from the Treasurer who said he didn't trust the Executive Administrator and suspected her of certain financial misappropriations. I asked him if he had any evidence to support this accusation, but he said he did not, just suspicions based on inconsistent monthly financial statements. The situation called for an ethical decision: Should I ignore the issue? Or try to resolve it as soon as possible?

I chose to bring these two together to discuss the matter immediately. I knew they were both committed to the organization and told them I was grateful for their loyalty. It was their distrust for one another that I couldn't ignore. I assured them that if they continued to distrust one another, I would ask them BOTH to step down. Since neither person wanted this, they agreed to collaborate on their monthly financial statements and account for all money. Lack of trust could have destroyed this volunteer organization. If we couldn't trust ourselves with our own money, how could anyone trust us with theirs?

Case 4D: Lack of Respect (pillar #2)

As President of a volunteer board, I had the responsibility of appointing committee chairs, and I asked one board member to chair the organization's Website Committee. As such, she had to work closely with the Chief Information Officer (CIO) who would report to her. Soon thereafter I learned that she didn't want to work with him, meet with him, or even hold Website Committee meetings at all. She believed her role was simply to tell the CIO what to do and make sure he followed orders. He, on the other hand, took offense because he felt the chair made arbitrary decisions, ignored team input, and lacked respect for his IT expertise. Should I ignore the issue? How could I possibly resolve the conflict?

I called a private meeting with both parties. Although the committee chair wanted to leave after one hour, she stayed for nearly three! In the end, they both agreed to a compromise: she wouldn't try to tell the CIO what to do, and he wouldn't report to her. Both kept their autonomy. When it came to the organization's website, they agreed to collaborate on website recommendations only and leave it up to the board to make decisions. Although they never held another Website Committee meeting, they did work together on making recommendations to the board.

Case 4E: Lack of Responsibility (pillar #3)

During my first term as President of this volunteer board, one board member volunteered to start a LinkedIn group for the organization. Since social media was a new undertaking for the board, we authorized him to go ahead — for the sole purpose of announcing organization-sponsored events. The trouble began when he started using the LinkedIn group to promote his own business events. We had a strict privacy policy agreement with members; LinkedIn gave him instant access to members' email addresses. Instead of accepting responsibility for their right to privacy, he chose to use the addresses for his own purposes. Despite warnings from the board, he continued to send out announcements, sent from the organization's group account and bearing the organization's logo. Question: Once a board member has been given responsibility for a task and abuses it, what can the Board of Directors do to solve the problem?

First, we gathered the evidence, including each of the personal mailings he had sent out using the organization's group account. Then, we distributed copies of these to the board and asked this board member to give his side of the story. He was contrite and claimed it had been done in error. Unfortunately, his lack of responsibility and lack of credibility couldn't be restored by his apologies, nor could the board trust him with managing the organization's LinkedIn account. They voted to reassign this responsibility to a paid staff member. The problem was solved.

Case 4F: Lack of Fairness (pillar #4)

Volunteer boards must have the moral courage to stand on the core ethical values of justice and fairness. When justice and fairness are compromised, the organization loses its credibility, financial support declines, and board members resign. I experienced all of this during my final term on one volunteer board. The primary cause of the injustice was the concealment of a memo written by members of a regional consortium and addressed to our Executive Administrator with explicit instructions, "Please read to your board." She did not. She didn't want the board to see the resentment and disruption that the name change was causing with members of this regional consortium. We only learned of the existence of the memo when a consortium member asked if the Executive Administrator had read the memo they had faxed to us. She had not. Only emails *favoring* the name change had been distributed to the board; negative comments had been suppressed and withheld from the board.

The situation called for moral courage. I believed that deliberately concealing information from board members was unjust, unfair, and downright dishonest. According to Josephson, "fairness implies adherence to a balanced standard of justice without reference to one's own biases or interests."[21] When confronted with the lack of transparency, the Executive Administrator said that the current President had instructed her NOT to read the consortium's memo to the board. Regrettably, the Executive Administrator had chosen to follow orders and act on her own interests, rather than demonstrate moral courage and do the ethical thing. As the truth unfolded at the board meeting, I finally asked the question, "Doesn't anyone see a problem here?" The room was silent. Only two people had the moral courage to speak up: the Senior Vice President said he objected to having his email intercepted, and the Treasurer said he objected to the lack of transparency. The Treasurer then made a motion that the Executive Administrator "forward on Fridays any and all emails addressed to all board members for that week." The motion passed unanimously. I believe that concealing information from your board is a sign of deeper, more intrinsic problems; your board isn't committed to core ethical values.

Case 4G: Lack of Caring & Lack of Citizenship (pillars #5 and #6)

Founded in the 1950s, this volunteer board had a history of donating a small college scholarship to one high school graduate annually, but it had no history of philanthropy. It held an annual sporting event, but after expenses, all proceeds went into the operating budget. As the newly elected President, I called upon the board to act on its mission, which stated: "This volunteer board is organized to advance the general welfare and prosperity

---

[21] Josephson, 12.

of the region so that its citizens and its business community may prosper. All reasonable means to secure these ends may be exercised. Particular attention and emphasis shall be given to the business, social, civic, cultural, and educational interests of the region."

Question: Besides donating a small scholarship once a year, how could we demonstrate that we were giving *"particular attention and emphasis to the business, social, civic, cultural, and educational interests of the region?"*

Answer: We needed our stakeholders to see — by increasing our community outreach and visibility — that we were acting on our mission and were committed to the core ethical values expected of volunteer boards, in particular "caring" and "citizenship" (Josephson's core values #5 and #6 respectively). When a group of community-minded citizens and I proposed a new community-outreach program to raise money for the local veterans' park, bring the business and civic communities together, and help citizens in need, the board voted as follows: 16 yes, 1 no, 4 abstentions, and 4 non-voters. In short, only a slim majority of 64% voted to support this community-outreach program and its goals. It came as no surprise to me, then, that they voted to cancel this very popular program two years later because, as one board member told local papers, "The program required months of planning and organizing, focusing solely on the township. We're a regional organization, representing over 90 communities in the region. Going forward, we want to move towards hosting more regional events."

On the contrary, the focus of this community-outreach program had never been "solely on the township." The focus had always been on our mission and commitment to core values — responsibility, caring, citizenship, and philanthropy. Instead of delivering on this promise, the funds raised from the last year of the program went into the board's operating budget; the funds did not go to support "the business, social, civic, cultural, and educational interests of the region" as stated in the organization's mission.

Every board needs to commit to its mission by acting on it. You need to repeat your mission statement *proudly and often* to your board members. You need to tell the press exactly HOW the actions of your organization reflect your mission and values. You need to demonstrate your mission and values to ALL your stakeholders. Don't leave it up to them to figure out. You need to shout it from the rooftops!

A second attempt at promoting philanthropy with this organization was more successful. I asked two dedicated committee chairs to work together to form a non-profit Foundation whose purpose was as follows:

> The Corporation is organized exclusively for charitable, religious, educational, and scientific purposes under section 501(c)(3) of the Internal Revenue Code, or corresponding section of any future federal tax code. The Corporation shall facilitate the accomplishment of those charitable, religious, educational, and scientific objectives of this organization, which are properly covered under section 501(c) (3) of the Internal Revenue Code, or corresponding section of any future federal tax code.

These two committee chairs, along with two other board members who served as officers of the Foundation, demonstrated remarkable moral courage in getting the non-profit Foundation off the ground. They stood on their principles, upholding IRS rules and regulations and insisting that every dollar raised during the dedicated special event go directly to the charity. They defended their core ethical values. They made me proud to call them colleagues and friends.

Case 4H: Lack of Trustworthiness (pillar #1)

According to ethicist Josephson, "Moral courage is the engine of integrity. It is our inner voice that coaxes, prods, and inspires us to meet our responsibilities and live up to our principles when doing so may cost us dearly."[22] Serving on a volunteer board during a time of discord can help you discover just how difficult living up to your principles can be.

During her quarterly report, the Executive Administrator of this volunteer board proudly announced that she had written an article for an upcoming journal publication. I knew her statement wasn't entirely true. The first draft had been written by her intern. Then she revised his draft but wasn't satisfied with it, so she asked the Marketing Committee, which I chaired, for assistance. At this point, her draft still lacked sufficient

---

[22] Michael Josephson, "Commentary 847.4: Moral Courage –The Engine of Integrity," *What Will Matter*, 2 October 2013, <http://whatwillmatter. com/2013/10/commentary-moral-courage-the-engine-of-integrity-801-4/>.

content, footnotes, organization, or branding required for publication. After considerable research and rewriting, only a couple of her original sentences remained; nevertheless, she kept the byline. The situation called for an ethical decision: Should I ignore the issue? Or listen to the inner voice telling me to say something about who the real authors were? I chose not to say anything at the board meeting because I didn't want to embarrass the Executive Administrator in a public forum.

Ideally, the Executive Administrator should have explained to the board that she had asked the Marketing Committee to assist with writing the article, and I believe the board would have respected her honesty. But instead of divulging the truth, she took credit for the work of others. In retrospect, I should have reached out to the Executive Administrator and asked her to change the byline to include all contributors, but I didn't act on that inner voice, the one coaxing me to "live up to my principles." Then, if she still took credit for the article, we could have reported the incident to the Executive Committee who did her performance reviews, telling them that the article had been ghostwritten by others, but she had taken full credit. In retrospect, I wish I had acted on the inner voice coaxing me to tell the truth and not be an enabler. Instead, I did nothing to help her tell the truth or be more trustworthy. I wish I had remembered that morale courage requires that we be "leaders in the service of truth,"[23] as Sister Thomas defined it.

Case 4l: Lack of Fairness (pillar #4)

If your bylaws are unclear about how your organization nominates and elects officers, be prepared for trouble. Just and fair elections are critical for healthy organizations. During my last term on this volunteer board, I learned that the bylaws hadn't been updated for nine years and many of them weren't being followed. When it came to appointing a Nominating Committee for the upcoming election, the Executive Administrator simply asked for volunteers and empowered them herself! The importance of selecting a Nominating Committee is emphasized in the *Standard Code of Parliamentary Procedure*:

---

[23] "Our Mission: Servant Leadership at U-Mary."

> A nominating committee is one of the most important committees of an organization because it can help secure the best officers.... A nominating committee should be a representative committee. Many organizations provide, for example, that if the nominating committee consists of five members, three of the five members are elected by the membership, and the chairman and the fifth member are appointed by the governing board.[24]

Past experience on other boards had taught me the importance of just and fair elections, so I was dismayed when I learned that the Executive Administrator had appointed the chairs of the Nominating Committee, Bylaws Committee, and others. What's more, none of these appointments had been voted on or approved by the board! The impropriety of these appointments was further evidenced in the organizations bylaws, which stated that the Executive Administrator "shall not be a member of the board." How could someone who wasn't even a member of the board appoint committee chairs? *Roberts Rules of Order* says that actions such as this are improper: "Motions that conflict with the corporate charter, constitution or bylaws of a society, or with the procedural rules prescribed by national, state, or local laws, are out of order, and if any motion of this kind is adopted, it is null and void."[25] The situation called for an ethical decision: Should I ignore these improprieties? Or at the very least, let the board know what was going on?

I chose to speak up and let the board know what was going on. This practice was unjust and unfair to everyone involved: to the Chairman, to the board, and to the volunteers serving on these new committees. At a special meeting prior to the election, I explained to the board that we needed to avoid any appearance of impropriety in our election procedures. I reminded them that the Executive Administrator wasn't a member of the board and, as such, had no authority to appoint committee chairs. We needed to ensure that we were following our bylaws and all guidelines from

---

[24] Alice Sturgis, "Selecting a Nominating Committee," *The Standard Code of Parliamentary Procedure*, 4th ed., (New York: McGraw-Hill, 1966) 152.

[25] Henry M. Robert, "Improper Motions," *Roberts Rules of Order Newly Revised*, 10th ed. (Cambridge, MA: Da Capo Press, 2000), 332, lines 15-18.

our parent organization, including this one: "The Chairman of the Board appoints the chairs of the councils and committees."

The newly appointed chair of the Nominating Committee was quick to defend his position saying that in the past, committee chairs had been appointed by the Executive Administrator, not the governing body. True. However, non-compliance in the past doesn't justify non-compliance in the present! I believed we needed to comply with our bylaws, guidelines from the parent organization, and *Roberts Rules of Order.* Period.

How could this board solve the problem? According to the board *Handbook*, "The Chair should hold the Executive Administrator accountable for meeting the goals of the board and serving its public purpose." Clearly, the Chairman of the Board had the authority to tell the Executive Administrator not to appoint committee chairs. Since she wasn't a member of the board, she had no authority to do so, no matter how long the practice had been going on. Likewise, the Chairman of the Board had a responsibility to ensure that this board was in compliance with its bylaws, guidelines from the parent organization, and *Roberts Rules of Order.* Unfortunately, he resigned before any ballots for his re-election could be cast, and the Executive Administrator was never held accountable.

Caution: If your board is planning an election, you need to make sure your bylaws are up to date and that they include just and fair nomination and election procedures, plus a clear statement of who has the authority to appoint committee chairs. If not, you risk having the entire election declared "null and void."[26]

In summary, moral courage is that inner voice that coaxes you to live up to your principles and make ethical decisions, even if doing so could cost you dearly. Moral courage and servant leadership are values still being taught at some universities, where "Learners become leaders in the service of truth." Moral courage is what's needed when pressures in your organization or workplace threaten to compromise your values and principles. If you want to mobilize, direct, and motivate volunteers, then you will be called upon to act on your "core ethical values" as ethicist Michael Josephson calls them:

1. Trustworthiness
2. Respect

---

[26]   Robert.

3. Responsibility
4. Fairness
5. Caring
6. Citizenship

All of the situations described in this chapter — from dealing with deception and conflicting values to dealing with discord — required making ethical decisions based on these "Six Pillars of Character." The best volunteer boards are those whose members aren't afraid to speak up and, when presented with unethical behavior, have the moral courage to take action.

CHAPTER 5

Change

"Change is the law of life. And those who look only to the past or present are certain to miss the future."

--John F. Kennedy

Lesson 5: Board members must be open to change

Rigid leaders — incapable of adapting to new ideas, new information, or changing times — can destroy volunteer boards. When you first volunteered, you probably hoped that you could make a difference. No doubt you were eager to present your ideas, make suggestions for improvement, and help move the organization forward, right? Instead, were your suggestions rejected even before you had a chance to explain them fully? Were you treated like an outsider? Or made to feel as though you were trespassing on someone else's territory? Unfortunately, territorialism is all too common in volunteer organizations. To be effective, volunteer boards must not only listen, but also RESPOND to new ideas, new members, and potential new leaders. If not, members won't feel as though they are being heard or valued at all. Handled properly, brainstorming sessions can help cultivate new ideas, engage new members, identify new leaders, and help build consensus. Most important, they can help volunteer organizations create a less rigid and more relaxed atmosphere — one that shows you value new ideas and are open to change.

Case 5A: Adding Value to Membership

Soon after I was elected President of a volunteer board, the outgoing President met with me and advised that if this noble organization, which had just celebrated its 50th anniversary, was going to survive for another 50 years, it needed to offer more benefits to its members. In his words, "we need to add value to membership." I agreed, but how?

I was reminded of a similar experience in the 1970s with Sister Gwendolyn, U-Mary Alumni Director, when we formed the university's first Alumni Association. To create this new organization, we had to figure out why someone would want to join. What were the benefits of membership? Sister Gwendolyn sent me out to interview some graduates to get their ideas and input. I have used this "bottom-up" approach in every organization that I have ever led. Instead of telling people why we thought they should join, we asked THEM to tell us. Like Sister Gwendolyn, I believe that when members are engaged in the creative process and are being asked to generate ideas (no matter what the topic) they are more likely to own them. And, they are also more likely to volunteer to help implement them.

So how could this volunteer board "add value" to membership? This was the question I posed to a small group of members who volunteered to brainstorm with me. At our first brainstorming session, I papered the walls with blank sheets of paper and handed out a questionnaire for them to do some pre-writing and idea generating before we started the discussion. Every single one of their ideas got written on the walls, and every single person had a chance to speak. I paraphrased each idea as I recorded it on the blank sheets to ensure comprehension and clarity; no idea received praise or criticism. I had used this group process successfully with college faculty and other organizations so I was familiar with the process. The key question was: *Why are you a member?* The answers and their testimonials (see **Table 2**) came easily to the group.

Table 2. Results of Brainstorming Session, 2009: Ten Reasons to Join

Benefit	Testimonial
Networking	"For the past 13 years my business has grown, thanks to member networking."
Credibility	"Even though we have hundreds of members, it still feels like being part of a community. Our membership sticker is proudly displayed on the front door of our business."
Visibility	"We get exposure. We get to meet businesses around the community and are able to make ourselves known among the businesses."
Advertising	"Advertising opportunities in this volunteer board are a great way of getting your name out there!"
Recognition	"The newsletter gives members a chance to be recognized for their successes, and it gives us a chance to tell them about ours."
Education	"Having fellow members participate in my sales workshops has enabled me to share timely business development tips, and it has led to new and meaningful business relationships."
Services	"It's very important for business people to help other business people, especially in these times."
Involvement	"When I joined this organization, I wanted to meet other business people and become involved in the community. You have helped me accomplish both."
Fun	"Our goal was to have a dedicated, special event that was 'bigger and more fun' than ever before. The event was sold out – and then some!"
Bottom Line	"Thanks to membership in this volunteer board, our non-profit has been able to tap into financial resources that we could not have reached without your assistance."

This personal, "bottom-up" approach proved invaluable in helping this organization identify the benefits of membership. What's more, it demonstrated that we valued their ideas and respected their honesty. In fact, using members' own words provided the content and outline for a slide presentation, an advertising flyer, and even a page on the website called, "Ten Reasons to Join," which is still being used today.

Case 5B: Negativism

Negativism is defined as "a habitual attitude of skepticism or resistance to the suggestions, orders, or instructions of others" and is characterized by "persistent refusal, without apparent or logical reasons, to act on or carry out suggestions, orders, or instructions of others."[27] Negativism will destroy brainstorming sessions and the group process, so it is critical that all participants withhold judgment, especially at the idea-generating stage of the process. As group facilitator, it was my responsibility to enforce this rule. Of all the participants, the Executive Administrator found it the most difficult NOT to criticize the ideas of others. She wasn't comfortable with this bottom-up approach. She was used to implementing her own ideas. This may have been the first time that the volunteers had more power than she, and it seemed to unnerve her. Unlike Sister Gwendolyn, this Executive Administrator had little tolerance for ambiguity. She didn't think that brainstorming with our members would produce results — just more work for her.

This organization needed to engage the Executive Administrator without giving her more work to do. Once I convinced her that I would take responsibility for facilitating the brainstorming sessions, for typing up the results, and for limiting the number of tasks recommended by this ad hoc committee of volunteers, she was more cooperative.

Caution: If your Executive Administrator doesn't support the processes or changes you recommend, you will reduce your chances of success. Consider how the changes you recommend will affect the Executive Administrator, the staff, and the budget. Do your homework. Be prepared to persuade (or even lobby) your fellow board members to support the changes you propose. Keep in mind that you will gather more votes in your favor if you volunteer to do the work or lead the effort to implement the changes.

Case 5C: Rigidity

If you have ever served on a volunteer board, very likely you have encountered rigid, inflexible attitudes and resistance to change. Rigidity

---

[27] "Negativism," *The Free Dictionary*, 2014, <http://www.thefreedictionary.com/negativism>.

in organizations is characterized by "the inability to change or be changed to fit changed circumstances."[28] Like negativism, rigidity will prevent your volunteer board from implementing change. I can relate. Soon after this volunteer board elected me President, I discovered that the Executive Administrator's stiff, authoritarian nature had earned her the nickname, "the sergeant at arms" primarily because of the rigid, military-like manner in which she handled people at events. One new member, a high-profile business executive, remarked, "The Executive Administrator yelled at me because I was sitting at the wrong table. She embarrassed me in public. I left and will not be renewing my membership." Unfortunately, this member's first impression was so negative that no matter how I apologized, I couldn't get her to reconsider. This Administrator's rigid seating plan, nitpicking details, and verbal criticism cost us a member who never came back. How true the adage is: "You never get a second chance to make a first impression."

If your Executive Administrator is inflexible, resistant to change, or (even worse) militaristic, you need to address the problem before your members do! Why are some people so afraid to change? I found this explanation particularly helpful:

> Tied closely to the need for *perfection,* the fear of change promotes anxiety about not getting things right. It makes sense that the best way to avoid the pain of failing is not to do anything at all. Yet failure is the only way to succeed. Think of Edison's failed light bulbs before the one that worked. Successful business owners have a list of failed attempts behind them. It's the way we learn.[29]

As a business owner and entrepreneur, I have my own list of failed attempts and have learned the value of making mistakes. To be an effective President, I knew that I had to address the Executive Administrator's perfectionism, fear of failure, and resistance to change. She was used to

---

[28] "Rigidity," *The Free Dictionary,* 2014, <http://www.thefreedictionary.com/rigidity>.

[29] Susan M. Heathfield, "Resistance to Change Definition," *About.com,* 2014, <http://humanresources.about.com/od/glossaryr/g/Resistance-To-Change-Definition.htm>.

being in control, so I suspected that fear of losing control was actually causing the problem. We needed to talk. To reach her, I knew I had to start by building this woman up, not criticizing her. So in an initial performance review I accentuated the positive: (1) she was *valued and loved* for always taking care of the details, (2) she was *appreciated* for always protecting the organization from potential failure, and (3) she was *admired* for always controlling the perceived chaos! In short, I used honey, not vinegar, to assuage her fears and recruit her cooperation. As Sister Gwendolyn would say, "She needed to know that I honestly cared about her as a human being." It was a good starting place for building mutual respect and trust. Moreover, since I would be doing her performance reviews, I reminded her that mutual respect and trust would be critical for her advancement. Disrespect and distrust would no longer be tolerated.

To address her fear of change, I asked her to ask herself, "What's the worst thing that could happen?" For example, if someone sits at the wrong table, what's the worst thing that could happen? I used this question often with her, just as I've used it myself whenever I've been afraid to change or to be changed: "What's the worst thing that could happen?" The answer is never as bad or tragic as you fear. Try it and see for yourself.

Case 5D: Communicating with Stakeholders

Soon after I joined another volunteer board, I was asked to chair its Marketing Committee and was given the responsibility of communicating with our stakeholders via print, media, and the Web. Developing a new website was my top priority, followed by print collateral and press releases to all of our internal and external stakeholders. We desperately needed to increase our visibility, but first I had to find out WHO the official spokesperson for the organization was.

Does your organization have a written policy regarding who speaks to the press? If not, you need to establish one. Until I asked this question, I assumed the Executive Administrator was the official spokesperson for this volunteer board. Not so. I found the answer in the "roles and responsibilities" statement distributed by the parent organization, which clearly stated, "The Chairman of the Board acts as the organization's public spokesperson."

Case 5E: Turf Wars

In healthy organizations, the leaders willingly accept their roles and responsibilities; in this one, the Executive Administrator did not. She refused to accept the authority of the Chairman, whom the parent organization had deemed the "spokesperson" for this board. Rather, she believed she was the spokesperson and had no intention of relinquishing this role which she had assumed for years. Consequently, when the Marketing Committee tried to write a new policy statement (consistent with guidelines from the parent organization that the Chairman of the Board act as public spokesperson), she simply never let the document out of committee! As a result, the board never got a chance to discuss, review, or vote on it. The Executive Administrator simply refused to relinquish her "spokesperson" role; she refused to change.

Volunteer boards are notorious for this type of "territorialism" or "turf war." A turf war is an argument between people who each want to control a particular area[30] or seek to obtain increased rights or influence.[31] In the case above, the *primary* turf war was between the Chairman and the Executive Administrator who believed it was her responsibility to speak to the press, not the Chairman's. The *secondary* turf war was between the Marketing Committee and Executive Administrator who believed it was her responsibility to create and set policy, not theirs.

To be effective, volunteer boards must be prepared to define their roles and responsibilities and then abide by these definitions. In the case above, the Chairman of the Board should have moved the communications policy statement out of committee and presented it to the entire board for discussion, review, and vote. The entire board needed to take charge of the situation by: (1) making it clear to the Executive Administrator that her attempt to suppress committee recommendations wouldn't be tolerated, (2) informing her that her refusal to follow policies and standard operating procedures would be noted in her performance review, and (3) holding this Executive Administrator accountable for her non-compliance. Instead,

---

[30]   "Turf War," *Macmillan Dictionary*, 2014, <http://www.macmillandictionary.com/thesaurus/british/turf-war#turf-war_4>.

[31]   "Turf War," *The Free Dictionary*, 2014, <http://www.thefreedictionary.com/turf+war>.

nothing was done to assert the Chairman's "turf" or role as spokesperson; he resigned. Nothing was done to create a communications policy; the committee fell apart. The Executive Administrator stayed; she refused to change.

Case 5F: Power Struggles and Sabotage

During the time I served on this volunteer board, one of the most active committees was a committee led by a very independent, bright, and talented business executive who was committed to improving the organization. He worked closely with the Executive Committee and donated many hours to developing a strategic plan for improvement. After months of hard work and due diligence, he arranged to share his findings at a special presentation for all internal stakeholders. As an attendee, I was stunned by what transpired. His presentation was sabotaged by two other board members. They took issue, not with WHAT was being said but with WHO was saying it, stating that that the Executive Administrator should have been involved in, not excluded from, the development of the report.

No matter how well-intentioned a committee chair is, when a power struggle exists between a committee chair and the Executive Administrator, you can expect fireworks. In this case, the fireworks took the form of sabotage. Because the Executive Administrator hadn't been involved in committee meetings and her name didn't appear on the report, some board members took offense. When they saw they had an opportunity to confront the committee chair in public, they were ready and waiting for their attack. The result? This volunteer was blindsided in public, his many hours of dedication and hard work were undermined, and his ideas for improving the organization never got implemented. He resigned a few months later. In the power struggle between the committee chair and the Executive Administrator, the Executive Administrator had won, but the organization lost a leader — and an extraordinary volunteer.

Woodrow Wilson once said, "If you want to make enemies, try to change something." This was certainly true in the case above. Excluding the Executive Administrator from his committee not only challenged her power and authority, but also alienated her from this important and valuable committee. But rather than resolving this conflict privately, she chose a public forum to sabotage him. Nothing was resolved by this spiteful act. I believe that both parties could have solved the problem if they had done two things differently.

First, the Executive Administrator should have delegated authority to this committee chair and trusted him to get the job done. After all, she knew that he was working closely with the Executive Committee and had the expertise required to do the strategic plan. Instead, her insecurities caused her to try to micromanage him and his committee. When that failed, she escalated to lobbying other board members to support her, and ultimately they sabotaged his presentation. Lesson learned: Whenever you delegate authority to volunteers, you must avoid trying to control every step of the process or dictate HOW the assignment should be completed. Instead, checking in after an agreed upon interval, such as at the mid-point of the project, would be a much more effective way of monitoring performance.

Second, the committee chair should have made an effort to engage the Executive Administrator in the work of this committee (if only as an observer) and keep her in the loop via periodic status reports and/ or meeting minutes. The lack of communication and exclusion from committee meetings only maximized her resistance to his efforts. Another lesson learned: When a change is introduced with a lot of discussion and member involvement, resistance to change is minimized.

Case 5G: Adherence to Tradition

The success of any organization depends on the effectiveness of its leaders. Unfortunately, most volunteer organizations don't have a budget for training leaders, and this volunteer board was no exception. Soon after my husband and I volunteered, we realized that it was struggling to find leaders, recruit members, and promote the organization in general. To survive and compete with so many other extracurricular activities for youth, we thought it needed some "revitalization." We offered suggestions to help. What we didn't anticipate was how reluctant this organization would be to listen to, yet alone implement any of the changes we suggested.

According to one source, traditionalists have a "tendency to submerge individual opinions or creativity in ideas or methods inherited from the past."[32] The members of this volunteer board were traditionalists; they had a tendency to glorify the past, especially the 1960s, when the organization had many more members and much more public funding. By the time we joined in the 1990s, budgets had been drastically cut, including staff salaries. The Program Coordinator, an hourly employee and senior citizen, said she didn't have any more hours to give to the organization. To her "revitalizing" simply meant more work, and she told us that volunteers (who weren't her boss) had no right to expect more work from her. The President, a young man with incredible loyalty to the organization, said he was just a volunteer (not her boss), and didn't have the authority to hire more help or any budget to implement new ideas.

To assuage their fears, I offered my *pro bono* services as a trainer and project manager to get the revitalization effort off the ground. I believe what happened next is a common experience on volunteer boards — even though I was the newly elected Vice President, I was made to feel as though I was trespassing on someone else's territory. Simply put, they valued their traditions more than they valued revitalization.

I drew upon my success with the U-Mary Alumni Association and College Writing Council to develop a revitalization and training program for club leaders. I recommended starting with a questionnaire, aimed at identifying grassroots issues the leaders wanted to address. Then I planned to follow up the questionnaire with a process workshop for leaders, giving them an opportunity to listen, express their vision for this organization, and infuse it with new ideas, strategies, and action steps. My proposal was unanimously approved by all 8 leaders present at the September 2003 leaders' meeting.

We are all creatures of habit. We like our routines and don't like to be faced with uncertainty. But staying in our comfort zone — especially when it comes to volunteer boards — can be detrimental to the health of an organization. This Program Coordinator, when faced with uncertainty, preferred to adhere to tradition and stay in her comfort zone. And, to stay in her comfort zone, she believed she had to dead-end the revitalization efforts. First, she called club leaders and told them NOT to fill out the questionnaire but to say instead, "Everything is fine the way it is." Second, one hour before the October leaders' meeting where the results of the

---

[32] "Traditionalism," *The Free Dictionary*, 2014, <http://www.thefreedictionary.com/traditionalism>.

survey were to be presented, she arranged an ambush-style emergency meeting with the Regional Director, aimed at halting any efforts to discuss the survey. Third, she asked leaders NOT to attend the process workshop because "Everything is fine the way it is."

Ultimately, I was able to distribute the questionnaire (see **Table 3**) and hold the process workshop, but the workshop was attended by only 8 of 18 leaders, as well as the Program Coordinator and Regional Director whose presence severely limited the attendees from speaking freely.

Table 3. Questionnaire for Volunteer Board

Topic	Question
Volunteers	1. How does this organization listen to its **volunteers**?
	2. What action steps could we take to be better listeners to your ideas, comments, and suggestions?
Parents	3. How does this organization listen to **parents** of our members/youth?
	4. What action steps could we take to be better listeners to parents?
Members/Youth	5. How does this organization listen to its **members/youth**?
	6. What action steps could we take to be better listeners to members/youth?
Other Comments	7. Are there any other comments you'd like to make?

Why was the Program Coordinator so opposed to this volunteer-led, grassroots initiative? Unlike Sister Gwendolyn, this Program Coordinator was threatened by our feedback; she didn't want to hear from any of the stakeholders, preferring instead to remain in her comfort zone. Even worse, I believe she was afraid the truth would get out. And it did. When I made follow-up calls to club leaders, I learned that many of the clubs no longer existed. In truth, there were only 18 active club leaders, not 31. By inflating the numbers for some time, the Program Coordinator had been misleading the organization (and the Regional Director) into believing it was nearly twice the size it was and, consequently, that her workload was nearly twice as demanding. Even worse, she didn't want anyone to know (especially the

Regional Director) that the organization needed improvement. The idea of revitalizing the organization definitely rocked her comfort zone.

Despite her objections (and at my own expense), I mailed the questionnaires to the 18 active leaders; 13 of them (72%) responded with helpful and constructive comments, and 5 of them declined to fill it out saying, "Everything is fine the way it is." I typed up every response and distributed the survey results so everyone knew they had been heard. In spite of the Program Coordinator's objections, I believe this grassroots initiative was the right place to start.

Does your organization care about its members? Do you want to know what you could be doing to make your organization better? If so, start with a questionnaire, make some follow-up calls, and conduct a process workshop. Don't be afraid to step out of YOUR comfort zone. This Program Coordinator couldn't stop us; in fact, the following year she left the organization.

Case 5H: Refusal to Alter the Status Quo

Resistance to change is "the act of opposing or struggling with modifications or transformations that alter the status quo in the workplace."[33] Fear of change is one of the most common reasons for resistance to change because it stops you from taking any action at all. Once again I experienced real "resistance to change" when I tried to get this volunteer board to change the way it registered projects for the annual exhibition. If your organization has ever tried to move from paper to email, you know what I mean! To register any project for the exhibition (and some children had as many as 20 projects each), every project had to be listed by hand on a sheet of paper and faxed to the office. Then, on the morning of the exhibition, every project needed to have a project label filled out — by hand and in duplicate — and taped to the project. It took hours to do all this last-minute paper work. The expense of printing paper forms and the inefficiency of writing the same information three times needed a solution. However, the Program Coordinator didn't want to "alter the status quo" and change the way registration had always been done.

Sometimes civil disobedience is the only solution to overcoming resistance to change! In the case of this volunteer board, I simply refused to

---

[33]   Heathfield.

comply with these outdated, time-consuming registration procedures and developed something more efficient and postage-free. I used my computer to create a sheet of identical exhibit tags (4 tags on a sheet) that could be emailed to all my club members. If a member planned to enter 16 projects in the exhibition, he/she could simply print out 4 sheets, fill in the tags, and tape them to each project BEFORE bringing them to the exhibition. No need for filling out labels at the event. Emailed or faxed to the office before the exhibition, these sheets of tags also served double-duty as the member's registration, thus eliminating an entirely separate and duplicative registration process.

What was the Program Coordinator's response? On the morning of the event, she and her Program Assistant demanded that we rewrite every tag (over 100 of them) for every project before it could be entered! Why? Because our tags weren't written on perforated paper like theirs so they couldn't tear them in half! I handed each of them a pair of scissors. Problem solved. When the other leaders saw how the sheet of computer-generated tags streamlined the registration process, they wanted a sheet. Years later, this sheet of exhibit tags is still being used to register AND label projects for the annual exhibition.

In sum, I think Charles Darwin's comment on natural selection is relevant here: "It is not the strongest of the species that survives or the most intelligent that survives. It is the one that is the most adaptable to change." Like the human species, if your volunteer board wants to survive, it must be "adaptable to change." People express their lack of adaptability in many ways: negativism, rigidity, turf wars, power struggles, sabotage, adherence to tradition, and refusal to alter the status quo. The lesson I learned from Sister Gwendolyn is that if you *ask* the members of your volunteer organization for their input, if they feel heard, and if feel they feel valued, they are more likely to adapt to proposed changes.

Sister Gwendolyn also impressed me by the way she introduced new policies, procedures, and suggestions for improving our fledgling Alumni Association. Not only did she listen to every member's suggestion, but she also *responded* personally to them. Impulsive, surprise attacks weren't her style. Communication was key. She took the time to investigate how the proposed change would affect ALL stakeholders, those who would endorse the change as well as those who would object. Handled properly, brainstorming sessions, questionnaires, grassroots initiatives, and process workshops can help you identify and understand stakeholder feelings, cultivate new ideas, engage new members, identify new leaders, and help build consensus. Most important, they can help volunteer organizations create a less rigid and more relaxed atmosphere — one that shows you value new ideas and are "adaptable to change." When it comes to volunteer organizations and life in general, Sister Gwendolyn and I would agree with John F. Kennedy, "Change is the law of life. And those who look only to the past or present are certain to miss the future."

CHAPTER 6

Accountability

"A body of men holding themselves accountable to nobody ought not to be trusted by anybody."

--Thomas Paine

Lesson 6: Board members must be held accountable

If your organization doesn't send out an agenda before each board meeting, then be prepared to have your time wasted. Likewise, if your meetings take longer than two hours, examine the reasons why. No one appreciates dull, boring, unproductive meetings. Whether you serve on the board or on a committee, you need to hold your leaders accountable for their performance, in particular the way they handle meetings, since this is the most direct way they interact with members. Who evaluates the officers and committee chairs? Who evaluates the organization's Executive Administrator and staff? A real warning sign for a dysfunctional board is lack of accountability. If the board members aren't really "minding the store," and you have no procedures to prevent misuse of authority, don't be surprised if you have trouble recruiting or keeping board members. Poor leadership — and lack of accountability for it — can reduce your membership faster than you can control the exodus.

One of the advantages of working with Benedictine nuns for so many years was seeing firsthand how they held each other accountable for living out their day-to-day commitment to each other and to their religious community. Their founder, St. Benedict, a keen observer of human nature, stressed the importance of the person and the relationship of persons living together. In his Benedictine community, or "school for the Lord's service"[34] as he described it, everyone must accept responsibility for the outcomes expected of them — both good and bad. Coming from a family with 13 children, my parents had created a similar *atmosphere of accountability*. We knew that our actions, both good and bad, affected everyone and, therefore, we were accountable to everyone. We took this responsibility very seriously, looked out for one another, and kept each other in line. Volunteer boards could learn much about accountability from large families and religious communities.

For example, according to *The Rule of St. Benedict*, the abbot is directed to "arrange everything that the strong have something to yearn for and the weak nothing to run from."[35] When I worked with Sister Gwendolyn as an Alumni Association volunteer, she directed our organization with a similar philosophy; that is, she gave the strongest members "something to yearn for" and the weakest members "nothing to run from." This *humane approach* to personal relationships guided her life, her leadership style, and our organization. This chapter contains several examples of volunteer boards that struggled to create an *atmosphere of accountability*. I suggest several *humane approaches* for holding members accountable for their actions. It focuses specifically on organizations struggling with responsibility, trustworthiness, liability, and answerability.

Case 6A: Struggling with Responsibility

Accountability has been defined as "an obligation or willingness to accept responsibility or to account for one's actions."[36] If you are the President of a volunteer board, you have several obvious responsibilities. For instance, you must send out meeting notices with a meeting agenda, start and end meetings on time, keep accurate financial records, ensure accurate minutes of all proceedings, and engage board members in voting and

---

[34]   "Prologue," *The Rule of St. Benedict in English,* ed. Timothy Fry et al (Collegeville, MN: The Liturgical Press, 1982) 18, line 45.

[35]   "Chapter 64: The Election of an Abbot," *The Rule of St. Benedict in English*, ed. Timothy Fry et al (Collegeville, MN: The Liturgical Press, 1982) 88, line 19.

[36]   "Accountability," *Merriam-Webster Dictionary,* 2014, <http://www.merriam-webster.com/dictionary/accountability>.

decision making. If you aren't doing these things, then you are NOT being responsible. Likewise, board members also have responsibilities. For instance, you must show up on time, stay until the end of the meeting, be prepared to vote on whatever is expected of you, review financial records, and ensure accurate records of all proceedings. In addition, you are often expected to volunteer for at least one committee or task force and donate your time, talent, and/or treasure by making a financial contribution to the organization.

Soon after being elected Vice President of this volunteer board, I noticed that the President never sent out an agenda. The staff would email the meeting notice, but there was never any agenda attached. Furthermore, the President usually arrived late to board meetings. During the meeting, he typically called on the Secretary to read the minutes of the last meeting and on the Treasurer to give the financial report, but the rest of us seldom were involved in any decision making, strategic planning, or voting, usually because there was no quorum present. I surmised that after dozens of years with this same President, same officers, and the same pattern of inactivity, people had simply stopped coming to meetings because they were a waste of time. Is it any wonder that these board meetings often had to be cancelled and rescheduled due to lack of attendance?

Case 6B: Poor Attendance at Board Meetings

Poor attendance at meetings was merely a symptom of more serious issues with this board: (1) The President had become irresponsible and complacent but didn't want to give up his power or title. (2) The Treasurer, a senior member of the organization, had complete control of the checkbook and didn't want to give up her power or title either. (3) Since the officers had no desire to give up their titles (and the organization had no bylaws, term limits, or other members interested in running for office), the members of the board just kept re-electing the same officers — year after year. And, this pattern of indifference, poor attendance, and irresponsibility just kept on going — year after year.

First, this board needs to stop ignoring the situation and hold the President accountable for his tardiness and complacency. Meetings should start on time. A President who is always late is irresponsible and a poor role model. A President who never sends out a meeting agenda is equally irresponsible. In short, this dysfunctional board needs a new President!

Second, the Treasurer should engage board members in all financial discussions. Spending decisions should be made by majority vote, not by the Treasurer alone.

Third, these board members should step out of their comfort zone and take responsibility for their own indifference. They could begin by defining the roles and responsibilities of their officers, committee chairs, and board members. One of the most humane ways to do this is to work with a team to brainstorm what they need from their officers and then communicate these needs to everyone involved. I provided several suggestions for defining roles and responsibilities in Chapter 2, including committee charters (**Figure 3**). What else could this board do? I strongly recommend that they create an *atmosphere of accountability* by heeding the advice of St. Benedict: "arrange everything that the strong have something to yearn for and the weak nothing to run from." If they did this, perhaps their attendance might even begin to improve.

Case 6C: No Expectations Defined

Because this volunteer board did not have clearly defined expectations for anyone involved (including board members for that matter), it had become so dysfunctional that people stopped coming to meetings. At last report, it was still blaming budget cuts and staff turnover on dwindling attendance and lack of participation. When things don't go right, the natural tendency is to find excuses or blame someone else for the situation. These are not useful responses. The real problem with this board was its complacency. Instead of defining expectations and holding everyone accountable, they had chosen to do nothing. In short, no one was "minding the store."

This board should stop blaming budget cuts and staff turnover for its own missteps and take responsibility for its stagnation. Everyone needs to accept responsibility for the outcomes expected of them — both good and bad. They need to look out for one another and keep each other in line. How could they begin to create this atmosphere of accountability? First, this board needs to "call the whole community together" (as Sister Gwendolyn's might say) to determine the wisest course. *The Rule of St. Benedict* provides excellent advice for summoning the brothers to counsel: "The reason why we have said all should be called for counsel is that the Lord often reveals what is better to the younger. The brothers, for their part, are to express their opinions with all humility, and not presume to defend their own views obstinately."[37] During a council meeting, the group needs to identify its weaknesses and celebrate its strengths. Once they have done this, they will be better prepared to define expectations for everyone in their board "community." This kind of honest dialogue has been missing from this organization for way too long.

Case 6D: Struggling with Trustworthiness and Liability

Liability is defined as "the state of being legally responsible for something, such as the payment of money for which a person or business is legally responsible."[38] Whenever a volunteer board engages in fundraising, it must be accountable for donating the money to the cause for which it is intended. Good fundraising requires accurate bookkeeping, trustworthy reporting, and a committed team of fundraisers. The absence of any one of these qualities can spell disaster for your board.

During my two-year term as President of a volunteer board, the largest fundraisers we organized were a community-outreach program (portion of proceeds donated to a charitable organization) and an annual sporting event (all proceeds donated to the organization's non-profit Foundation). During both of these fundraisers, we struggled with trust and liability issues.

Case 6E: Finger Pointing and Blaming

In any fundraising effort, it is critical that the Executive Administrator (often the person collecting the checks) and the Treasurer (the person balancing the books) trust one another. In this volunteer board, they did not. The lack of trust between these two individuals spelled disaster. How could we expect the public to trust us with their donations if we didn't trust ourselves? We needed to find a way to build trust and hold them accountable for their actions.

---

[37] "Chapter 3: Summoning the Brothers for Counsel," *The Rule of St. Benedict in English*, ed. Timothy Fry, OSB, et al (Collegeville, MN: The Liturgical Press, 1982) 25, lines 3-4.

[38] "Liability," *Merriam-Webster Dictionary*, 2014, <http://www.merriam-webster.com/dictionary/liability>.

To help build trust, I looked for some project that would require their collaboration, an activity that would be highly visible to the board and to the public in general — a project that would help stop the finger pointing and blaming and require teamwork. I considered a community-outreach program, a highly visible project that would hold them accountable for recording every penny raised and every penny spent. We had an ambitious, eight-week media plan for the program; I assured them that the media would be watching our every move. I assigned them key roles and told them that I would no longer tolerate any financial discrepancies, finger pointing, or blaming.

First, I had the Executive Administrator accompany me to the Town Council meeting to help present our program proposal and get their blessing to proceed; I introduced her to everyone as the critical "project facilitator." Second, I had the Treasurer accompany me to a Township Committee meeting to go over the proposed budget and our fundraising plans; I introduced him as the project's critical "Certified Public Accountant." As donations for this community-outreach program came in, these two people were in the spotlight for maintaining accurate financial records and reporting all revenues and expenses to the board. I believe that bringing them together, giving them important responsibilities, and elevating their profiles not only helped elevate their self-esteem, but also increased their accountability and willingness to work as a team. In the end, they both seemed happier and their finger pointing and blaming ceased.

Case 6F: Workplace Bullying

If the President of your volunteer board ever admits, "I don't trust anyone," be prepared for trouble. This is what the newly elected President of one volunteer board said to me soon after her election. She had just gone through a difficult personal situation, so I attributed her distrust to this. Without trust, though, I knew she would have a difficult time leading this volunteer board, but I definitely wasn't prepared for the disastrous chain of events that followed. Her aggressive, tyrannical behavior resulted in the largest exodus from the board and its Foundation that it had ever experienced.

When a President distrusts her own board members, the fuse is lit and the fireworks are inevitable. Here are some of the fireworks we experienced on this volunteer board: (1) This President often didn't allow debate at board meetings, cutting people off saying, "no discussion," as though to show her dominance over them. (2) Lacking trust and respect for certain board members, she wouldn't delegate authority to them, as though to show her superiority over them. (3) This President seemed to fit the behavior of bullies: "they turn to being powerful in a way that they feel brings them respect. They feel that being feared is the way to gain respect and surround themselves with friends and people who look up to them."[39]

The four people this President seemed to distrust and target the most were the Senior Vice President, the Vice President of the sporting event, and two other officers on the organization's non-profit Foundation. All four of these individuals were well-educated, high-profile leaders in the community who were deeply committed to the philanthropic goals of the organization. However, unlike Sister Gwendolyn, this President didn't try to lead by example and model appropriate workplace behavior; she demanded obedience and instilled fear. She frequently used telephone bullying to criticize and personally insult some board members. She also made a point of excluding these four people from critical discussions and decision making. To make matters worse, because she didn't trust the Foundation Treasurer to keep accurate records, she comingled Foundation donations with other revenues, creating significant liability issues for the organization with the IRS. Did this board hold her accountable for any of these actions? No, they did not, and according to today's psychology experts, "Saying nothing is almost as bad as committing the bullying act itself."[40]

If your board has a tyrant or bully in a leadership role, you need to take immediate and decisive action to stop this behavior. If not, the aggressive behavior could worsen and turn off even more members and donors. To manage the situation, consider these options:

Option 1: Reconciliation. I recommend that you call a special meeting of your board to discuss the problem. Make sure you have a record of dates and specific examples of the offensive behavior. Recruit an impartial, third-party mediator (such as your board's legal counsel) to lead these discussions. If the offending person refuses to acknowledge his/her behavior or to

---

[39] "The Psychology of Bullying," *Theravive*, 2014, <http://www.theravive.com/research/The-Psychology-Of-Bullying>.

[40] "The Psychology of Bullying."

reconcile with the people involved, then be prepared to make a motion calling for the person's resignation. The majority vote of the board should rule.

Option 2: Filing a Grievance. If you haven't already done so, develop a policy and Standard Operating Procedure (SOP) for filing a grievance in your organization — whether it be a staff member, an officer, committee chair, board member, or any other member of your organization. Most boards do NOT have such an SOP or even a Grievance Committee because they don't anticipate difficulties. I recommend that your board establish a policy on workplace bullying so you can take action, when/if necessary (see **Table 4**). Consult your board's legal counsel to help you formulate a policy for promoting a respectful workplace.

Table 4. Sample Policy on Workplace Bullying

Section	Description
Policy	The dignity of the human person is intrinsic to this organization and to our mission. It is the policy of this organization to value, respect, and promote the self-esteem and dignity of every person involved in it — staff, Executive Administrator, officers, committee chairs, board members, and the general membership. The board is encouraged to be vigilant to any and all bullying messages and behavior.
Definition of Workplace Bullying	Workplace bullying is a pattern of repeated physical, verbal, psychological or social aggression that is directed towards a specific individual by someone with more power and is intended to cause harm, distress, and/or create fear. Bullying of any form or for any reason can have long-term physical and psychological effects on those involved, including bystanders. Bullying may be carried out overtly (e.g., face-to-face) or covertly (e.g., through repeated social exclusion or via technology). It is a sub-category of aggression and is different to, but also related to, harassment and violence. It is not the same as conflict or social dislike even though, in some cases, the outcome of both can be bullying. Some recognized forms of workforce bullying are:[53] - frequent yelling or verbal abuse, alone or in the presence of others; - frequent ridicule or being put down; - persistent and unjustified criticisms, especially if they involve petty, irrelevant or insignificant matters;

[41] "Standard Operating Policy: Promoting a Respectful Workplace: Preventing and Managing Workplace Bullying," Ambulance Service *of New South Wales, 18 July 2012,* <http://www.ambulance.nsw.gov.au/Media/docs/Promoting%20a%20Respectful%20Workplace%20Preventing%20and%20Managing%20Workplace%20Bullying,%20July%202012-7a69e8d8-5881-41fe-8aca-ba1b3be40dd5-0.pdf>.

	- spreading gossip, malicious rumor, or innuendo about a person with an intent to cause the person harm (including psychological, emotional or physical harm); - inappropriate disclosure of personal / confidential information about a person to others; - repeated threats of disciplinary action for no good reason; - insults based on a person's appearance, race, gender, sexuality; - humiliating a person through inappropriate gestures, sarcasm, criticism or insults; - any form of cyber bullying, including leaving offensive messages or images on a person's computer; - offensive telephone messages; - using offensive objects or images in order to embarrass or humiliate; - deliberately sabotaging a person's work; - interfering with someone's personal property or work equipment for no valid reason; - excluding or isolating a person from workplace activities; - lodging frivolous, vexatious, or otherwise mischievous grievances about an employee; - deliberately altering work arrangements to inconvenience a particular employee or group of employees; - setting unreasonable deadlines or tasks; - encouraging other people to participate in bullying behavior.
Procedure for Filing a Grievance	The Grievance Committee of this board is responsible for reviewing reports of workplace bullying. Your report should include sufficient information such as details of dates, times, and witnesses that might assist the Committee to assess the level of seriousness of the matter. You can get a copy of the confidential form for filing a workplace grievance from the Chair of the Grievance Committee and/or our legal counsel. The Grievance Committee will arrange a meeting with you to discuss the grievance. If necessary, more than one meeting will be held. A decision on the grievance will be confirmed in writing within 7 working days of the grievance meeting. If you are not happy with the outcome, you may appeal the decision in writing to entire board. The decision at that stage will be final.

During this President's one-year term, her bullying behavior never ceased. Fortunately, she resigned after only one term. Unfortunately, by that time so had the Senior Vice President, the Vice President of the sporting event, the entire Foundation board, and many other long-standing and talented board members. Regrettably, the remaining board members said nothing and did nothing to hold this President accountable for her actions, and (this quote is worth repeating), "Saying nothing is almost as bad as committing the bullying act itself."[42]

Case 6G: No Policy for Evaluating Work Performance

The lack of accountability on boards is one of the most common, insidious problems that any board faces. As you know, the higher your expectations and accountability, the more likely you are to get improved results and higher morale. On the other hand, the lower your expectations and accountability, the more likely you are to get poor results and lower morale. Without accountability, your board could easily be victimized by a tyrant, or you could experience the other extreme — someone who doesn't want to do very much at all and isn't answerable to anyone. The latter was a serious issue for another volunteer board on which I served.

For many years the Executive Administrator of this volunteer board had no supervision. She had a job description, but no one seemed to know exactly what it was. She was her own boss, choosing her favorite tasks and ignoring others. She was a political appointee with many political allies on the board, and she had no intention of answering to the President, the Executive Committee, or anyone else who tried to hold her accountable for her performance. Once this happens, it is difficult, if not impossible, for a board to pull back the reins. Although the parent organization had published a clear definition of the "roles and responsibilities" of the Executive Administrator, this person had no intention of following that definition saying, "They are only guidelines, not requirements." To make matters worse, this board had no policies or procedures in place for measuring her performance or the performance of her staff who were also salaried employees.

First, if your board doesn't already have a Standard Operating Procedure (SOP) for performance appraisals (one that explains who, what, when,

---

42 "The Psychology of Bullying."

where, how, and why performance appraisals will happen, as shown in **Table 5**), you need to develop one. Keep in mind that your ultimate goal is to get positive results, close performance gaps, maintain good relationships, and permanently resolve problems. Second, someone on your board needs to meet privately and annually with the person(s) being evaluated, keeping all reviews confidential. Third, your board needs to make sure that recommendations for merit increases are fair and/or that the agreed upon performance gaps have been closed. You need to resolve performance problems and make people answerable for their performance on your board, no matter what the person's position, temperament, or power.

Table 5. Sample SOP for Performance Appraisal

Standard Operating Procedure	
Policy	It is the policy of this organization to conduct performance appraisals as a means for discussing, planning, and reviewing the performance of each salaried employee.
Purpose	The primary purpose of performance appraisal is to identify how well employees are doing their work and how they can improve their performance. Performance appraisal can also be used in determining salary increments; as a factor in determining order of lay-offs; as a basis for training and promotion, demotion, transfer or dismissal; and for other purposes as set forth in regulations.
Period of Evaluation	All newly appointed and promoted employees, except temporary workers, shall be evaluated at the end of three months of service, and annually thereafter. Employees shall also be evaluated at the time of separation (exit interview).
Merit Increase	An employee shall not be eligible for a merit raise until the performance appraisal has been completed.
Evaluation	Performance appraisal reports shall be prepared by each employee's immediate supervisor and reviewed by the Chairman of the Board or his/her designee. A supervisor who is leaving his/her position may be required to prepare performance appraisal forms on all those employees under his/her supervision who have not yet been evaluated within the previous six months.

Standard Operating Procedure	
Review with Employee	The Chairman of the Board or his/her designee shall discuss each performance appraisal with the employee being evaluated. If an employee disagrees with any statement in an appraisal, he/she may submit, within ten days following the conference with his/her supervisor, a written request for review through the chain of command. If an employee still disagrees with the evaluation, he/she may file a grievance.
Confidentiality	A performance appraisal shall be confidential and shall be made available only to the employee evaluated, the supervisor(s) involved, the Chairman of the Board and/or the governing body's Chief Administrative Officer.
Authority	The Executive Board has the authority to change, modify, or approve exceptions to this policy at any time with or without notice. Last reviewed: March 24, 2013

Case 6H: No Performance Reviews

I think most boards don't formally review the performance of their salaried employees because they don't know they have the responsibility or power to perform this function. Moreover, most Executive Administrators and staff aren't likely to suggest that the board evaluate them because, according to one source, "It's important to recognize that *when we make ourselves more accountable we always lose power* — at first. That is because we are handing over power to others so that they may judge our actions."[43] No wonder people don't want to be evaluated! Beware: Doing nothing isn't a solution; it can perpetuate poor performance.

The first step in creating an atmosphere of accountability is to develop performance appraisals for all salaried employees on your board. Don't exclude them from the development process; ask for their ideas. If possible, solicit their help in brainstorming ways to overcome ability barriers. Bring in peers to share ideas, and listen carefully to their suggestions. Don't let employees off the hook by trying to blame others or claim that their hands

---

[43] "Accountability in Teams," *Talent Technologies*, 15 November 2012, <http://www.talent-technologies.com/new/2012/11/accountability-in-teams/>.

were tied. An accountable leader is willing to admit that he or she needs advice or knowledge, but here's a word of caution. According to *Harvard Business Review*, the ability to admit weakness seems to be lacking in today's workforce:

> The youngest members of the workforce, especially in the US, have grown up in a sheltered environment; they expect praise and recognition and can be indignant when it is not forthcoming. They are not particularly open to critical feedback. No surprise, then, that at a time when talent retention and engaging employees is *de rigueur* we get silly advice from management such as, "don't give employees a hard time about their weaknesses, celebrate their strengths."[44]

A second consideration: Keep in mind that some employees may not be open to critical feedback. However, if you really don't like something they have done, you need to tell them why and suggest some solutions to correct it. Do you risk hurting someone else's feelings? Yes, but according to some experts, "that is a risk, but a greater risk is in being untruthful. We do not control how another will take what we say. As long as we are saying it in the most loving and caring way possible, if they allow it to hurt them, then that is on them. A leader must be truthful and honest with their words."[45]

A third step in creating an atmosphere of accountability is to figure out the barriers to employee success on your board and then set milestones, target dates, and metrics to help keep them on track. Waiting until after the fact will only increase their frustration and yours. Every board needs to develop a humane and respectful way to evaluate work performance, one that is aligned with its mission and values. Here is excellent advice from one source:

---

[44] Darren Overfield and Rob Kaiser, "One Out of Every Two Managers is Terrible at Accountability," *Harvard Business Review*, 8 November 2012, <http://blogs.hbr.org/2012/11/one-out-of-every-two-managers-is-terrible-at-accountability/>

[45] Henry E. Shade, "Accountability in Leadership," *Innovision Global*, n. d., <http://myemail.constantcontact.com/Newsletter-from-Innovision-Global-.html?soid=1109342299024&aid=RchNMb-7PVk>.

While accountability is a must in any organization, it should be balanced and enhance the concepts of vision, innovation, transparency and learning. When we hold ourselves and others accountable, as leaders, we show that we have a mutual respect for one another, which leads to an organization being more creative, efficient and effective and in turn leads to happy employees, which ultimately leads to happy clients/customers.[46]

Table 6 contains an example of a performance appraisal with a professional development plan for the Executive Administrator of a volunteer board.

---

[46]   Shade.

Table 6. Sample Performance Appraisal for an Executive Administrator

Responsibilities - Executive Administrator	
Major Areas of Responsibility	• Support the Board in the conduct of its work • Community Partnerships • Planning and Budgeting • Career Center Development • Performance and Fiscal Monitoring *Evaluation criteria encompass such standards as impact, timeliness, cost effectiveness, client satisfaction, accuracy, consistency, etc.*
Performance Competencies and Core Values	• Managing Execution • Building a Strong Organization • Business Development • Collaboration / Teamwork • Communication / Interpersonal Skills
Performance Review	
General Information	Name Date of Review Job Title Review Period

Section 1 – Major Areas of Responsibility		
Performance Rating Scale	4 Exceeds Expectations 3 Meets Expectations 2 Needs Improvement 1 Fails to Meet Expectations **N/A** Not Sure	
Primary Performance Expectations: Responsibilities/Goals	**Notes/Comments on Achievements and Areas for Improvement**	**Performance Rating**
Support the Board in the conduct of its work		
Community Partnerships		
Career Center Development		
Planning and Budgeting		
Performance and Fiscal Monitoring		
Section 2 – Performance Competencies and Core Values		
Competency Area	**Notes/Comments on Competency Areas and Suggestions for Improvement**	**Performance Rating**
Managing Execution		
Building a Strong Organization		
Business Development		

Collaboration/Teamwork: Uses diplomacy and tact to maintain harmonious and effective work relationships with co-workers and constituents; adapts to changing priorities and demands; shares information and resources with others to promote positive and collaborative work relationships; supports diversity initiatives by demonstrating respect for all individuals.		
Communication/Interpersonal Skills: Is able to communicate effectively and to influence others in order to meet organizational goals; shares information openly; relates well to all kinds of people; is able to speak well and write effectively.		

Section 3 – Overall Assessment

Summary Comments:	Overall Rating (check one): ____ Consistently Exceeds Expectations ____ Successful Performance ____ Unacceptable Performance
Employee Signature:	Date:
Optional Comments:	

Section 4 – Growth and Development Plan **TO BE COMPLETED BY EMPLOYEE**	
Strengths:	
Growth/Development Opportunities:	
What will the individual do?	
What can the manager do to support this?	

Section 5 – Performance Goals and Expectations **TO BE COMPLETED BY EMPLOYEE and SUPERVISOR**	
Employee: _____ Job Title: _____	Review Start Date: _____ Reviewer Name: _____
Goals for Next Review Period: **SMART Goal** *(Specific, Measurable, Attainable, Realistic, Timely)*	**Measurable Outcome:**

In conclusion, trust and accountability are critical for a healthy board. Key indicators of lack of accountability include poor attendance at board meetings, lack of meeting agendas, no board attendance policy, lack of defined expectations for anyone, finger pointing and blaming, bullying, lack of written policies and procedures for evaluating work performance, and no performance reviews.

What are some solutions for building trust and accountability? First, define the roles and responsibilities of your officers, committee chairs, and board members. One of the most humane ways to do this is to work with a team to brainstorm what they need from their officers, committee chairs, and board members and then communicate these needs to everyone involved. Engage as many people as possible in an honest dialogue to identify your weaknesses and celebrate your strengths. Hire a group facilitator to help you if you don't feel confident doing it yourself.

Second, if key board members admit that they don't trust one another, identify or create a project for them that requires collaboration and teamwork — an activity that is highly visible to the board and to the public in general. Increase their profiles and elevate their self-esteem by shining the spotlight on their teamwork and commitment to the organization. If this doesn't work, try bringing them together privately to reconcile their differences. If one of them still refuses or is a workplace bully, consult your legal counsel and take the matter to your Grievance Committee. Make it crystal clear to the parties involved that distrust and bullying will not be tolerated by the board whose policies and procedures will be enforced.

Finally, develop a humane and respectful way to evaluate work performance, one that is aligned with your mission and values. To do this, you need a written policy and procedure for employee performance appraisals. Effective performance reviews should include milestones, target dates, and metrics to help keep salaried employees on track. Why go through all this effort? Because holding ourselves and others accountable shows that we have mutual respect for one another and is likely to lead to a more creative, cohesive, efficient, and healthy organization.

CHAPTER 7

Appreciation

"Feeling gratitude and not expressing it is like wrapping a present and not giving it."

--William Arthur Ward

Lesson 7: Board members must be appreciated

Gratitude is formally defined as "a feeling and expression of thankfulness for the efforts of others that are costly to them and beneficial to us." What's most costly and valuable to volunteers? It's their TIME. Don't waste it; cherish it. Say "thank you" publicly and often. Small gestures of recognition and encouragement can go a long way to keep volunteers motivated, feeling happy, useful, valued, and loved. Effective boards understand the importance of giving special awards or "certificates of appreciation" to top performers. Not only do recognition awards provide positive reinforcement and incentive for others, but they also bring the top-level managers and volunteers together. Moreover, recognition ceremonies can provide positive, "good news" stories for your organization in the press and help enhance your board's image and reputation.

According to the Roman philosopher Seneca, "Wherever there is a human being, there is an opportunity for a kindness." Sister Gwendolyn had the same philosophy and took every opportunity to express her gratitude with kindness. She also understood that whatever the recognition was, it needed to be timely and appropriate for the volunteer's support. She generally had two types of recognition: *informal* and *formal*. Her informal types of recognition were thank you notes, letters of commendation, and acknowledgements from the podium. Her more formal recognition awards had specific criteria, and often involved larger, more organized events. As a recipient of the U-Mary Alumni Recognition Award, for example, I was deeply honored by this formal recognition and very proud of this accomplishment. Whatever the type of reward Sister Gwendolyn delivered, she made it perfectly clear to our Alumni Association that every volunteer's contribution was sincerely valued and deeply appreciated.

How does your board thank its volunteers? If you have no informal or formal recognition program, I encourage you to start one today. Demonstrating that you appreciate their time and effort is one of the best ways to motivate, engage, and retain volunteers.

Case 7A: No Clear Definition of Tasks

One would think that a political organization — where everyone shares common political beliefs and values — wouldn't have any problem motivating volunteers, right? Not so. This political organization struggled to motivate and recruit volunteers. Here are some reasons why.

Since this political organization had a very small budget, the officers knew that volunteers would be key to success and growth; however, they didn't have a clear understanding of which volunteers would be best suited for what task, nor were the tasks clearly defined. Instead of taking the time to survey the volunteers and identify their talents and preferences, the officers simply did most of the work themselves — from sending out meeting notices to fundraising. Sound familiar?

The first step in any volunteer recruitment effort should be to ask people this critical question: WHY would you like to be involved in this organization? Once you know what *motivates* your volunteers, you will be better able to match their motivation to the recognition/reward. Recognition is critical to any volunteer program because it contributes to morale, productivity, and retention. I agree with this source:

> Demonstrating concern for your volunteers, ensuring that the tasks and jobs they are assigned meet their needs, and recognizing their contribution, will only increase a volunteer's satisfaction and willingness to further participate in your organization.... If volunteers are given meaningful tasks and rewarded and recognized appropriately

for these, they will have a sense of belonging and a feeling of accomplishment. This in turn will result in productivity.[47]

Table 7 provides some suggestions for matching volunteer motivation with the appropriate, meaningful response from the board.

Table 7. Volunteer Motivation & How to Respond

If the volunteer's motivation is...	Then the board should do this...
To support a cause, mission, vision, or shared value	• Explain clearly and *often* to volunteers what your organization is doing to support its mission, vision, and strategic plans. Be specific. • Take a few minutes at board meetings to share success stories of how individual volunteers are making a difference. Be specific.
To share knowledge, skills, and experience	• Match the knowledge, skills, and experience of individual volunteers with meaningful tasks and committee assignments. Use results from volunteer surveys to identify individual talents and preferences. • Don't waste volunteer time on trivial tasks and unproductive committees. • Invite volunteers with special skills to give brief presentations or reports to the board.

---

[47] Cheryl Humphrey-Pratt, "Volunteer Recognition: Matching Motivation to Rewards," *RCVO @ Volunteer Alberta,* 2006, <http://volunteeralberta.ab.ca/varc/wp-content/uploads/2012/10/rcvo-volrecognitn.pdf>.

If the volunteer's motivation is...	Then the board should do this...
To gain influence, prestige, publicity, or unique achievements	• Invite new volunteers to brainstorming sessions with officers and committee chairs. • Recognize your most active volunteers publicly and *often* (e.g., at board meetings, during committee meetings, in newsletters, annual reports, and press releases if appropriate). • Introduce volunteers to people of influence. • Recognize volunteers with Certificates of Achievement or Appreciation. • Recognize retiring board members and significant contributors with plaques and photos in media outlets.
To network for business and career advancement	• Ask volunteers WHO the best referral is for their business. Share this information with all board members and follow-up by making the appropriate introductions. • Write letters of recommendation and/or offer to be a character reference.
To improve job opportunities and acquire new skills	• Introduce volunteers to possible mentors and coaches on your board. • Provide training opportunities for volunteers to help improve their professional skills (e.g., brownbag lunch-and-learn). • Offer an orientation session for new board members and provide training updates for all board members, complete with certificates of completion and appreciation.

If the volunteer's motivation is...	Then the board should do this...
To socialize with others	• Ensure that the volunteer is in a team setting and doesn't work in isolation. • Include a social component at board meetings to help volunteers get to know one another and the organization (e.g., casual introductions, a roll call question, or small group discussion based on questions written anonymously and drawn from a hat). • Provide recognition activities that have a social component (e.g., lunch with officers, awards ceremony with dinner).

Case 7B: Asking for Help and Then Rejecting the Work Product

This is a common problem on volunteer boards that are tightly controlled by Executive Administrators or officers who prefer to do everything themselves. They tend to micromanage the organization. They seldom delegate assignments, or once delegated, reject the volunteer's work product because they consider the person's effort inadequate, unnecessary, or duplicative.

For example, in this political organization, a volunteer was asked to provide table decorations, but when she arrived to put them out, she was told by the President that they wouldn't be used because the tables were too small to accommodate decorations at all. Ouch. Very bad planning on the President's part. When you ask a volunteer to do something, first make sure it is something that really NEEDS to be done. Another volunteer in this same organization drafted the organization's mission statement, but it was never discussed or voted on. Even worse, the author was never told why. This is a sure-fire way to destroy morale and lose volunteers! What's more, disgruntled volunteers are likely to complain to others. There is a lot of truth in this statement, "A satisfied, happy volunteer tells three others; a dissatisfied, unhappy volunteer tells 13 others."[48]

This board needs to say "thank you" to every single contributor, no matter what they think of the person's work product. A volunteer's contribution is like a holiday gift. Although it may not be exactly what you asked for, you shouldn't insult the giver by rejecting the gift. This organization would benefit from less control and a lot more kindness. Day-to-day volunteer recognition doesn't have to cost a lot or take a lot of time. It just has to be sincere. Some of the least expensive forms of recognition, for example, can be found on supermarket shelves. **Table 8** lists several symbolic, inexpensive ways to say "thank you" that have proven successful.[49]

Table 8. Inexpensive Ways to Say "Thank You" to Volunteers

Symbol	Message
Tree seedlings or flower seed packets	"Thanks for helping us grow"
Paper clips or a glue stick	"Thanks for holding us together"
M & M candies	"Thanks for being Marvelous and Motivated volunteers"
Lifesaver candies	"You're a 'lifesaver' for our organization"
Candy mints	"Thanks for helping us raise a mint"
Ruler or tape measure	"Your contributions are immeasurable"
Party whistles	"Let's celebrate our success"
Package of batteries	"Thanks for energizing us"
Stick of chewing gum	"Thanks for sticking with us [or with this project]"
Flashlight	"Your vision is our guiding light"

[48] Mary V. Merrill, "Recognizing Volunteers," *World Volunteer Web*, 27 September 2005, <http://www.worldvolunteerweb.org/resources/how-to-guides/manage-volunteers/doc/recognizing-volunteers.html>.

[49] Connie Pirtle, "Ask Connie: All Things Recognition," *Volunteer Today.com: The Complete Gazette for Volunteerism*, 2014, <http://www.volunteertoday.com/Connie.html>.

Case 7C: Volunteers Who Seek Recognition but Don't Produce

Have you ever worked with a volunteer who eagerly offered to do a task and then failed to follow through? Notwithstanding legitimate excuses (e.g., lack of time, family crisis, career responsibilities), you were probably very disappointed. And, if this person volunteered to lead the fundraising effort in your organization and then dropped the ball, you were probably in big trouble. This is what happened to me while I chaired this volunteer board's largest community outreach program.

What do you do when a key volunteer doesn't produce? Or vanishes without giving any excuses? Although you may feel like firing this person, terminating volunteers isn't a healthy way to run an organization. I believe there are more "humane" ways to handle the situation.

First, resist the temptation to get even. Second, schedule a private meeting with this volunteer. Reassure him/her that nothing said at your meeting will be blabbed to anyone else. Confidentiality and trust are key. Third, find out what motivated this person to volunteer in the first place (see **Table 7**). Once you understand this person's motivation and subsequent reasons for not following through, ask the volunteer to recommend a solution. This approach not only shows you respect the volunteer's generosity, but also allows him/her to come up with an alternative solution (or even a substitute). If the volunteer cannot recommend a solution, be prepared to suggest some solutions yourself and (optimally) get their agreement on how to proceed. **Table 9** suggests some additional strategies for engaging volunteers who don't produce.

Table 9. Strategies for Engaging Volunteers Who Don't Produce

If the volunteer...	Then try this...
Doesn't have the skills for the volunteer assignment yet seeks recognition	• Transfer the volunteer to a new position. • And thank the volunteer publicly for being committed to the organization and for offering to assist in so many different ways.
Doesn't understand how the organization works but is motivated to learn	• Provide more training or one-on-one mentoring. • Or assign the volunteer to "shadow" one of your high-performing board members.

If the volunteer...	Then try this...
Is burned out and no longer is motivated to do the work	• Give the volunteer a "sabbatical" and a chance to rest. • Or transfer the person temporarily to something that is less stressful and more personally rewarding. • Or swap this volunteer with another organization for a few months and let him/her learn some new tricks.
Is a senior citizen who can no longer do the work he/she once did	• Meet privately and confidentially to agree on how to proceed. • And always give retiring volunteers the honor they deserve so they can depart with dignity.
Doesn't participate on any committees and rarely attends board meetings	• Meet privately and confidentially to agree on how to proceed. Find out if they want to resign or stay. • If they choose to stay, have a list of committees prepared so you can sign this person up. • If they choose to go, give the volunteer the respect they deserve so they can depart with dignity.

I believe Sister Gwendolyn would agree that the strategies above are much easier to implement and much smarter than firing a volunteer. Keep in mind that a volunteer may be behaving inappropriately for a lot of reasons —reasons that may surprise you, make you feel more compassion or respect, and even help you forgive them. She would say that before you consider separating that person from the program, you should try some of the alternatives suggested above. And she would be right.

Case 7D: Volunteers Who Dominate Committees

One of the least productive committees is one where a single volunteer chooses to do just about everything. Sometimes it's the chair who is reluctant to delegate tasks, but more often it's a long-time volunteer who won't let go of a project or believes it's their life's calling. What are the warning signs? People like this often limit the size of the committee to 1-2 others, are reluctant to invite new members, and generally refuse to collaborate with other committees. When volunteers like this dominate and control a committee or project, new volunteers inevitably get turned off and walk away saying, "They won't let me do anything" or "They don't seem to need my help." Sound familiar?

If one of your volunteers is dominating and controlling a committee or project, there are several things you can do about it. Just keep in mind that the more you empathize with this person or group, the more likely they will be to cooperate and collaborate with you. **Table 10** provides a list of positive steps to help improve collaboration.

Table 10. Strategies for Improving Volunteer Collaboration

If some volunteers...	Then try this...
Don't invite others to join the committee	• Refer to your bylaws to find out who has the authority to appoint people to committees, and then • Have the President meet privately with this group, and explain what it must do to be in compliance with the bylaws and to fulfill the mission of the organization. The President must stress the need for collaboration and invite others to join the committee.
Say they don't need help and try to control every task	• Arrange a brainstorming session with the board officers, Executive Administrator, and this committee to discuss all the tasks to be completed by the committee, and then • Prioritize the tasks and suggest an "owner" for each one, making sure to assign new committee members to collaborate with returning members.

If some volunteers...	Then try this...
Complain that no one can do the job as well or as efficiently as they	• Have the committee compile a list of tasks completed last year, and then • Have them swap assignments for the coming year with the understanding that each new "owner" must collaborate with the previous owner to complete the task as well and as efficiently.
Discourage people from joining their committee	• Have the committee personally invite 2-3 new members from different disciplines and backgrounds to help develop a new committee charter (see **Figure 3**), one that emphasizes collaboration. • Encourage this new, collaborative group to socialize outside of the workplace. • Finally, recognize and celebrate their collaborative behavior and collective accomplishments.

Case 7E: Lack of Volunteer Recognition

Some volunteer boards can't seem to retain volunteers. This was my experience with a volunteer board on which I served for three years. Some of the members of this large board (40+ members) had been there for ten years or more, serving primarily as fiscal monitors of federal funds. At the time I joined the board, the Executive Committee was trying to infuse it with new volunteers by forming some new committees. As you know, volunteers are more likely to stay involved with your organization if they feel appreciated for the work they do. However, this particular board had no formal system in place to recognize the contributions of its volunteer board members.

As the new Marketing and Public Relations Chair for this volunteer board, I recommended that our committee initiate the first-ever awards program and keep an archive of recipients over the years. Our first step was to define various "degrees of recognition" as shown in **Table 11**. Candidates for various awards were then recommended by the Marketing Committee and approved by the Executive Committee. Presentations could either be public (e.g., at special events or at quarterly board meetings), or private, upon the discretion of the Chairman of the Board.

Table 11. Sample "Degrees of Recognition" for a Volunteer Board

Name of Award	Description	Nam & Title	Year
Emeritus Award	The Emeritus Award (matted and framed) is for distinguished service. This honorary award is given only to a few and denotes perpetual status of individuals who moved the organization to new heights as former key members on the Board. *Emeritus* does not necessarily indicate that the person is retired from all the duties of their previous position and may continue to exercise some of them if/when called upon.	J. Doe Chairman of the Board	2013
Board's Certificate of Appreciation	The Board's appreciation award (matted and framed) is for outgoing committee chairs (resignations). It should be reserved for this purpose.	J. Smith, Marketing Chair	2012
		M. Smith, Finance Chair	2013
Certificate of Commendation	This commendation (in a folder) is for extensive, recent committee work — above and beyond the call of duty. It should be reserved for this purpose.	B. Baker, Bus Manager	2012

Admittedly, some volunteers like to be publicly recognized, but for others it is embarrassing. To make recognition meaningful and personal, you may want to ask volunteers how they would like to be thanked.

Table 12 contains 52 suggestions for recognizing volunteers. For detailed descriptions of these ideas, visit the Baudville Recognition Resource Center at www.baudville.com.

Table 12. Ideas for Volunteer Appreciation[50]

Volunteer Appreciation Event Ideas
1. Celebrate National Volunteer Week
2. Treat Volunteers to Lunch
3. Host a Garden Party
4. Give Them Just Desserts
5. Put the Pieces Together
6. Arrange a Social Tea Appreciation Event
7. Celebrate the Holidays as a Team
8. Show Them They Make a World of Difference
9. Roll Out the Red Carpet
10. Throw a Volunteer All-Star Party
Volunteer Awards
11. Submit a National Volunteer Award Nomination
12. Apply for the President's Volunteer Service Award
13. Recognize Length of Service
14. Create a Volunteer of the Year Award
15. Present Certificate Awards
16. Create a Peer-Nominated Award
17. Give a Helping Hand Award
18. Nominate a Volunteer for an Award at Their Alma Mater
19. Present a Client-Nominated Award
20. Give a Personal Character Pin Award
21. Design a Behind the Scenes Award
22. Establish an Outstanding Volunteer Recruiter Award

---

[50] "52 Volunteer Appreciation Ideas eBook," *Baudville: The Place for Daily Recognition,* 2011, <http://www.baudville.com/Volunteer-Appreciation-Ideas-eBook-Baudville/pdfs>.

Volunteer Appreciation Gift Ideas

23. Create Your Own Bookmarks
24. Give a Packet of Seeds or a Plant
25. Serve Baked Goods from Staff Members
26. Design Your Own Note Cards
27. Buy a Gift Book of Volunteer Quotes
28. Make a Donation to the Charity of Their Choice
29. Plant a Tree in Their Honor
30. Personalize Tote Bags
31. Give a Gift Certificate for a Night Out on the Town
32. Give Personalized Leather Journals
33. Arrange for Relaxing Neck and Shoulder Massages
34. Create a Photo Album
35. Purchase Lapel Pins for Everyone
36. Give a Piece of the Organization
37. Dedicate a Brick or Decorative Landscaping

More Low and No-Cost Appreciation Ideas

38. Send a Card to Volunteers' Homes
39. Present a Certificate of Appreciation
40. Highlight Volunteers in Your Organization's Newsletter, Blog, or Facebook Page
41. Add a Note to a Candy Bar or Snack
42. Send an eCard to Say "Thank You"
43. Publically Recognize Your Volunteers at a Meeting
44. Sing the Praises of Your Volunteers in a Letter to the Editor
45. Laminate and Frame the Volunteer's First ID Picture
46. Dedicate a Parking Spot or Name a Meeting Room in Their Honor
47. Deliver a Handwritten Note of Appreciation
48. Give a hug, High Five, Fist Bump, or Handshake
49. Collect Donations from Local Merchants and Businesses
50. Spell Out Your Appreciation in Chalk
51. Wash Volunteers' Cars
52. Ask a Volunteer for Input

Case 7F: Poor Delegation of Tasks

One complaint I heard from a fellow volunteer on one board was that she had been on the board for years, had offered to work on marketing, but had never been given a single assignment. She was delighted when I asked her to do some copy editing for our new website. This volunteer, like all volunteers, needed to feel connected to the organization, and one of the best ways to do this was to have her complete a specific task, project, or group activity. Feeling valued and "connected" to an organization are essential for productivity.

This advice is worth repeating, "If volunteers are given meaningful tasks and rewarded and recognized appropriately for these, they will have a sense of belonging and a feeling of accomplishment. This in turn will result in productivity."[51] Where does task delegation begin? It should be the primary responsibility of committee chairs. And to be effective, your committee chairs must create meeting agendas that specify topics, presenters, and time allotted, as illustrated in **Figure 5**.

Meeting Agenda Template		
Team Name	Date:	Time:
Meeting called by:	Type of meeting:	Location:
Facilitator:	Note taker:	Timekeeper:
Invited:		
Please read:		Please bring:
Agenda Items	Presenter	Time Allotted
1.		
2.		
3.		
4.		
5.		
Other Information: Observers: Special Notes:		

Figure 5. Template for a Team Meeting

---

[51] Humphrey-Pratt.

If your volunteers know they will be a "presenter" on a particular agenda item or task at the next meeting, they are more likely to come prepared to report on tasks they have been assigned. Furthermore, if the committee chair recognizes and rewards volunteers appropriately for their work, they are likely to have a better sense of belonging and be more productive. This was certainly the case with the volunteer I described above. Once I engaged her in meaningful tasks, not only was she more productive, but she also enjoyed being part of the committee for the first time in years. More importantly, this board retained a very valuable and committed volunteer.

To conclude, every volunteer's contribution must be sincerely valued and appreciated. It doesn't cost a dime to say "thank you," and as this chapter illustrates, there are dozens of other ways to recognize and reward volunteers, both formally and informally. Once you know what *motivates* your volunteers, you will be better able to match their motivation to the recognition/reward. On the other hand, if your board has volunteers who don't produce or are dominating and controlling the group, they may be behaving inappropriately for a lot of reasons — reasons that may surprise you and even help you be more compassionate. Before you consider separating them from the organization, you might want to try some of the alternatives suggested in this chapter. The bottom line is this: recognition is critical to any volunteer program because it contributes to morale, productivity, and retention.

CHAPTER 8

Conflict Resolution

"Do unto others as you would have them do unto you."

--The Golden Rule

Lesson 8: Top-level managers must resolve conflicts

One of the least favorite responsibilities of being in charge is conflict resolution. When conflict goes unresolved, teamwork breaks down. To keep your organization working effectively, this downward spiral must be stopped as soon as possible, and stopping it often requires involving top-level managers as "peacemakers." To begin, the board must designate a respected person in authority as the "peacemaker" or arbitrator. This person could be a former President, the Board Chair, a local official, an impartial legal advisor, or even a tribunal of several impartial individuals unless, of course, one or more of these individuals is directly involved in the dispute and would have a conflict of interest. After both sides of the conflict are presented, the disputing parties must abide by the arbitrator's decision; otherwise there can be no conflict resolution.

If your organization has no grievance process or even a simple conflict resolution process, I urge you to get one in place — sooner than later. If not, your board's problems could develop into a full-blown mutiny! Having experienced a board mutiny firsthand, I can assure you that you don't want to let that happen. An organization that fails to resolve conflict is doomed. To be effective in resolving conflicts, your board must have a conflict resolution process in place, plus a healthy respect for the individuals who enforce it.

If you have ever been the leader of a volunteer board, you know that resolving conflicts often requires the *wisdom* of Solomon. I think Sister Gwendolyn would have said that it also takes *courage* to approach others with a sense of empathy, openness, respect for their perspective, and forgiveness. The two cases described below involved the Chairman and the Executive Administrators of two volunteer boards on which I served. I share these multi-party disputes with you in the event you are ever on a board where top-level managers are themselves involved in the conflict. When this happens, the role of "peacemaker" often shifts to members of the Executive Committee, the board's legal counsel, a mediator, or someone trained in conflict management who can bring all parties together and provide an opportunity for positive change.

Case 8A: Role of the Executive Committee

Most boards have an Executive Committee. According to one source, "The reason behind establishing an Executive Committee is to grant to a small but trusted group of officers the authority to make any critical decisions (usually reserved exclusively to the board) in between board meetings. It's not uncommon to give an Executive Committee almost all the power of the board yet make the committee's decisions subject to the board's ultimate approval."[52] When conflict erupts in an organization, the Executive Committee is often called upon to help resolve it.

Case 8B: Conflict over Term Limits for the Chairman of the Board

While I served on the Executive Committee of this volunteer board, the issue of term limits for the Chairman of the Board was raised by a board member who wanted a new chairman. Here is what the bylaw regarding length of terms for officers said:

> The term of office shall commence on July 1 and end on June 30 of the second year of office. Each officer shall hold the office for two years or until a successor shall have been duly elected and qualified. No officer shall serve more than two consecutive terms in the same

---

[52] C. Alan Jennings, "A Committee of Special Standing," *Robert's Rules for Dummies* (Hoboken, NJ: Wiley Publishing, 2005) 244.

position unless authorized by the vote of two-thirds (2/3rds) of the Board.

The debate over whether the long-standing Chairman of the Board could be re-elected or not occurred in June, just before the July election, when this Chairman was running for his sixth consecutive term (12 years). Since the Executive Administrator and some board members preferred another candidate, they used this section of the bylaws to advocate for the current Chairman's dismissal, focusing on the phrase, "no officer shall serve more than two consecutive terms in the same position," while others said he could serve again, provided he be "authorized by the vote of two-thirds of the Board." To resolve the disagreement over this eligibility issue, the Vice Chair called upon the Executive Committee to make a recommendation; the majority voted that he be allowed to run again and the July election be allowed to go forward.

However, the negative effects of this multi-party dispute were many. First, teamwork and cooperation broke down. Second, discussions turned into heated debate with recriminations flying back and forth. Third, conflicting agendas turned into personal dislikes. Fourth, individuals disengaged from their work, spending too much time and energy campaigning for their candidates. Finally, the downward spiral of negativity and recrimination became so intense that this benevolent and well-respected Chairman withdrew entirely from the election! In my view, the organization was the biggest loser.

In every work environment, as we try to manage situations in which we are significantly invested, conflict is normal and often predictable. However, "if we develop procedures for identifying conflicts likely to arise, as well as systems through which we can constructively manage conflicts, we may be able to discover new opportunities to transform conflict into a productive learning experience."[53] I believe this board could have transformed this multi-party conflict into a "productive learning experience" if it had done just two things:

First, the Executive Committee could have engaged a mediator to resolve the bylaws issue as well as to oversee the election. The mediator (the

---

[53] "About Conflict," *Academic Leadership Support: Office of Quality Improvement and Office of Human Resource Development*, n. d., <http://www.ohrd.wisc.edu/onlinetraining/resolution/aboutwhatisit.htm#whatisconflict>.

objective third party) is often the legal counsel on the board, or a consultant who is trained in conflict resolution, or an external professional mediator. The mediator guides the conflicting parties in considering alternative resolutions.

Second, this board needed a conflict resolution policy and procedure, especially since the conflict involved top-level management. While a conflict resolution policy may provide a first step in dealing with a complaint, organizations typically address such complaints with a policy and set of procedures specifically designed for that purpose. If your board has nothing in place to guide you, I suggest you start with an SOP for resolving board conflicts (see **Table 13**).

Table 13. Sample SOP for Resolving Board Conflicts

Section	Description
Policy	It is the policy of this board to promote open communication and foster a safe environment for addressing differences of opinions. All reasonable efforts will be made to assure that the management of a conflict meets the needs of all parties involved and occurs in an atmosphere of mutual respect and understanding.
Procedure	This Standard Operating Procedure was created for resolving board conflicts and for protecting all board members from retribution for raising legitimate complaints and concerns.
	Step 1: At least one of the parties involved in the conflict prepares a formal (written or oral) complaint to an appointed "Conflict Resolution Manager" (e.g., the legal counsel on the board, or a consultant who is trained in conflict resolution, or an external professional mediator) who will investigate the complaint and recommend a resolution.
	Step 2: The parties involved in the conflict meet as early as possible to identify the specific nature, scope, and degree of conflict. Adequate information regarding the conflict must be gathered from all parties before attempting a resolution.

Step 3: The Conflict Resolution Manager explains how confidentiality will be handled during this process. Discussion regarding issues of conflict must be confined to internal communications only, maintaining the highest level of confidentiality appropriate to the issue.

Step 4: Does the conflict involve top-level management?

- If *yes*, then the Conflict Resolution Manager brings the matter to the full board or Grievance Committee who recommends a resolution.

- If *no*, then the Conflict Resolution Manager invites one or two members of the Executive Committee to participate in the process in order to maintain confidentiality, respect for the individuals involved, and focus on the issues. In this case, the designated "Conflict Resolution Managers" will be the President and another board member with specific experience or training in conflict resolution.

Case 8C: Conflict over Executive Administrator's Role as Public Spokesperson

While the press isn't likely to telephone most board members and ask them for statements, they may call the President or Executive Administrator of your board. You and your Public Relations/Marketing Committee need to agree on who the public spokesperson is. If your board doesn't have a clear policy for who the public spokesperson is, then you need to develop one.

The problem I encountered on one volunteer board was that the Executive Administrator believed the role of public spokesperson was hers. However, according to written guidelines from the parent organization, the Chairman of the Board "acts as the public spokesperson and key link with local elected officials and local chief elected officials on policies and strategic directions." To me, this made logical sense since the Executive Administrator wasn't a voting member of the board; she was a salaried employee, and the bylaws said she wasn't a member of this board. Since your organization's spokesperson is going to be quoted in press releases and mentioned in your marketing materials, you will need to understand who the authorized public spokesperson is. Lack of clarity created confusion and conflict on this board.

If your organization has a parent organization, then ask them for advice and direction. Since the public spokesperson is highly visible and often quoted, the parent organization should have a written policy. If not, ask them to create one. For example, "It is the policy of this organization that the Chairman of the Board be the public spokesperson for this board." As a rule, parent organizations require that their policies, procedures, and guidelines be implemented consistently, thus giving you the authority you need to enforce them. If individuals still refuse to comply, then you have the right to bring the matter to their attention for resolution and/or disciplinary action.

Another option for resolving this type of conflict is to create your own communications policy, as we did for this volunteer board. This approach, however, lacks the authority of the aforementioned approach. Although we created the first-ever written policy for the organization (a positive change), it also required compliance, and the Executive Administrator wasn't compliant (a negative response). To be effective in resolving conflicts, your board must have a conflict resolution system in place (for example, see **Table 13**), plus a healthy respect for the individuals who enforce it.

My advice to every volunteer board is to use the "times of peace" in your organization to get your bylaws, roles and responsibilities, and conflict resolution processes in place. Otherwise, you won't be prepared for "times of war" when emotions run high and situations can quickly spiral out of control. If you don't have the time or inclination to write these documents yourself, then hire someone to help you. It may be the best investment you'll ever make.

Case 8D: Conflict over President's Authoritarian Leadership Style

Have you ever been on a board where the members circulated a petition to remove the President from office? I have. Not only did board members want to sign it, but also past presidents who helped build its reputation, membership, and history. I believe the underlying cause of the conflict was the president's authoritarian leadership style.

According to one source, authoritarian leadership is "a leadership style in which the leader dictates policies and procedures, decides what goals are to be achieved, and directs and controls all activities without any meaningful participation by the subordinates."[54] Typically, authoritarian leaders (also known as autocratic leaders) "construct gaps and build distance between themselves and their followers with the intention of stressing role distinctions."[55]

If the President of your organization has an authoritarian leadership style, you're in for a bumpy ride! Since decisions on boards are supposed to made democratically (after discussion, with participation, and by majority vote), board members will not respond well to an authoritarian leader who is controlling, bossy, and dictatorial, making decisions independently with little or no input from the rest of the group. For example, some of the tactics the President of this volunteer board used to stifle debate were: (1) to declare flatly that there would be "no discussion," (2) relegate discussion to a committee, or (3) table the debate all together.

To make matters worse, this organization had no parliamentarian, and its legal counsel seldom attended meetings or returned phone calls. As the gap widened between the President and the board, several members banded together, refusing to be stifled and controlled by an autocrat. By the time the petition to oust the President was circulated, the battle lines between sides had been drawn. Disagreement at meetings resulted in unresolved animosity among peers. The stage was set for a board mutiny.

Explosive situations like this need to be defused, or they will only get worse. An understanding of Kurt Lewin's "power styles"[56] (see **Figure 6**) may help to understand the problem above.

---

[54] "Authoritarian Leadership," *Business Dictionary.com*, 2014, <http://www.businessdictionary.com/definition/authoritarian-leadership.html#ixzz39pu9tlEf>.

[55] "Authoritarian Leadership Style," *Wikipedia*, 25 February 2014, <http://en.wikipedia.org/wiki/Authoritarian_leadership_style>.

[56] Kurt Lewin, Ronald Lippitt, and Ralph K. White, "Patterns of Aggressive Behavior in Experimentally Created 'Social Climates.'" *Journal of Social Psychology*, 10 (1939): 271-299.

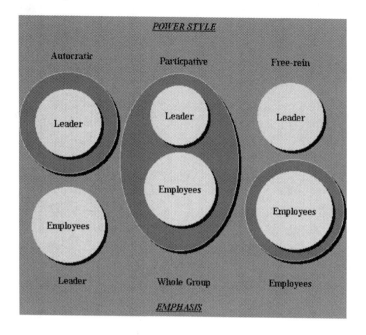

Figure 6. Power Styles

According to Lewin and his colleagues, leadership styles generally fall into three types: *autocratic/authoritarian, participative/democratic,* and *free-rein/delegative* (aka *laissez-faire*). Most sources agree that good leaders tend to use all three styles, with one of them normally dominant.[57] Bad leaders tend to stick with the one style of autocratic, as in the case described above. The darkest shaded area in **Figure 6** represents power, which for an autocrat is delegated entirely to the leader.

Why would the leader of this volunteer board choose an *authoritarian* or *autocratic* leadership style? I suspect that her leadership style had much to do with her profession and personality. As a Corporate Manager, she was accustomed to telling people what to do and how to do it, and apparently had been rewarded for this approach to problem solving. Perhaps she also feared that being more compassionate and trusting were signs of weakness. In any case, this autocratic style is never a good fit for a volunteer board

---

[57] "Leadership Styles," *Big Dog & Little Dog's Performance Juxtaposition,* 22 July 2014, <http://www.nwlink.com/~donclark/leader/leadstl.html>.

where the whole group expects to share power by participating in decision making.

When the leader's style is *participative* or *democratic*, the whole group shares power (as illustrated in **Figure 6**). This approach assumes that the leader doesn't know everything and would benefit from the input, knowledge, and skills of other board members. According to one source, "Using this style is of mutual benefit as it allows them to become part of the team and allows you to make better decisions."[58]

The *free-reign* or *delegative* leader (see **Figure 6**) is the opposite of the autocrat because, unlike the autocrat, the free-reign leader allows the members to make decisions and delegates most tasks to them. For this style to be effective, you must trust and have confidence in the people below you; that is, you must believe that they can analyze the situation and determine what needs to be one and how to do it.

Which leadership style would have helped solve the problem above? I believe this President could have defused this explosive situation with a more participative leadership style. Instead, her refusal to change her authoritarian style divided the board, prompted an exodus of board talent, and caused irreparable damage to the organization. Even in the face of a board mutiny, this President stubbornly refused to resign, holding firmly to her title to the end of her one-year term. She needed to develop ways of thinking and acting that were more consistent with the organization's values and behaviors. Instead of building bridges with board members — by promoting conciliation, collaboration, teamwork, and trust — she built up walls of hostility, antagonism, and distrust. In short, she needed to see that participative leadership wouldn't have been a sign of weakness, but rather a sign of strength.

Case 8E: Conflict over Executive Administrator's Role on Committees

An authoritarian Executive Administrator who insists on micromanaging every committee is nearly as destructive as an authoritarian President. If your bylaws don't spell out the responsibilities of the Executive Administrator, then you need to get that document written. Not only is this statement critical for the Executive Administrator's annual performance review, but

---

[58] "Leadership Styles."

also for your officers and committee chairs. Every board member needs to understand the Executive Administrator's role and responsibilities clearly.

The problem I encountered with this volunteer board was that the Executive Administrator, frustrated by the lack of consistent and effective leadership on its committees, attempted to micromanage everyone and everything. For example, she insisted that every committee and every subcommittee meet in her office; if she couldn't attend, the meeting was cancelled. As you can imagine, this inflexibility led to frequent conflicts and frustration on this board.

If your Executive Administrator has an authoritarian leadership style, then I have four recommendations:

(1) In order to foster a more democratic, participative atmosphere, the President needs to sit down with the Executive Administrator and agree on who does what, when, where, why, and how. There should be no confusion over roles and responsibilities for anyone *at any level* of the organization. Every board member needs to feel comfortable expressing problems and concerns — without fear of reprisal. Based on years of experience, I would agree with this source, "If such channels are perceived as closed, unsafe, and non-productive, they will be replaced by gossip, 'end runs' and back-biting."[59]

(2) If the President and Executive Administrator cannot agree on their roles and responsibilities and abide by them, then they need to ask an impartial advisor or mediator to help them get at the root of the problem. According to one source, "The mediator will help the conflicting parties in thinking of ways to assure that both of their interests will be met when arriving at a resolution."[60] As part of the resolution, the Executive Administrator's role on committees needs to be written down and agreed upon.

(3) If the Executive Administrator and the committee chairs cannot agree on their roles and responsibilities (or worse, refuse to collaborate), then the President or a neutral third-party mediator needs to get the arguing parties to come together and reach some type of agreement. To do this, they must show respect to each other, work together, and perhaps even

---

[59]   "About Conflict."

[60]   "Types of Conflict," *Conflict Resolution, Definition of Conflict, Conflict Management Styles*, n. d., <http://www.typesofconflict.org/>.

write or revise their committee's charter (see **Figure 3** in Chapter 2). Why a committee charter? Because the arguing parties are more likely to comply with an agreement that they helped to develop than one imposed on them.

(4) All the conflicting parties need to have a healthy respect for collaboration. To get to this point, they may benefit from an understanding of conflict management styles. One of the most popular models is the Thomas-Kilmann Instrument (TKI) for identifying conflict management styles, developed in the 1970s by Kenneth Thomas and Ralph Kilmann (see **Figure 7**). They argued that people typically have a preferred conflict resolution style. However, they also noted that different styles were most useful in different situations. They developed the Thomas-Kilmann Conflict Mode Instrument (TKI) to help identify which style you tend towards when conflict arises.

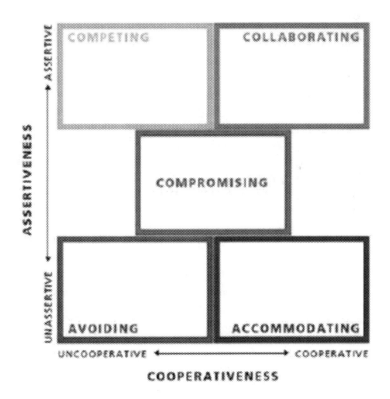

Figure 7. Thomas-Kilmann Conflict Modes

According to Kilmann, "Because no two individuals have exactly the same expectations and desires, conflict is a natural part of our interactions with others. The TKI is a self-scoring assessment that takes about fifteen minutes to complete. Interpretation and feedback materials help you learn about the most appropriate uses for each conflict-handling mode."[61] Their interpretation materials help conflicting parties understand the appropriate use of the styles and help them understand less familiar styles. The TKI can be quickly administered and interpreted, requiring about 15 minutes to answer the questions and about an hour for interpretation by a trainer.[62] **Figure 7** shows the five main styles of dealing with conflict which vary in their degrees of cooperativeness and assertiveness. Here is brief definition of each type of conflict resolution technique.

1. *Competing* (aka *forcing*): This highly assertive but uncooperative approach to conflict resolution is characteristic of people who firmly pursue their own concerns despite the resistance of the other person. Although forcing your view may provide a quick resolution to a conflict, it may also hurt your relationship with the opponent in the long run or cause the opponent to react forcefully too, even if the opponent didn't intend to be forceful originally.

2. *Collaborating* (aka *problem solving*): Collaboration is a highly assertive and cooperative approach to resolving conflict. With this method, conflicting parties attempt to work with one another to find a win-win solution to the problem, a solution that most satisfies the concerns of both parties. Collaboration is appropriate if a long-term, trusting relationship is important, but it may not be practical when timing is crucial and a quick solution or fast response is required.

3. *Compromising:* Compromising requires a balance of assertiveness and cooperation. People who compromise usually try to find an expedient and mutually acceptable solution to the conflict, one that

---

61   Kenneth W. Thomas and Ralph H. Kilmann, "An Overview of the Thomas-Kilmann Conflict Mode Instrument," *Kilmann Diagnostics: Dedicated to Resolving Conflict throughout the World*, 2014, <http://www.kilmanndiagnostics.com/overview-thomas-kilmann-conflict-mode-instrument-tki>.

62   Thomas and Kilmann.

partially satisfies both parties. This approach can be effective when the parties don't know each other well or haven't yet developed a high level of trust, but it can also result in a lose-lose situation if neither party is satisfied with the outcome.

4. *Avoiding* (aka *withdrawing*): This approach is both unassertive and uncooperative. People who avoid conflict don't pursue their own concerns or those of the opponent. They don't address the conflict or try to solve the problem; instead, they sidestep, postpone, or simply withdraw. In my experience, too many board members choose this approach. Usually it's because they don't want to deal with hostility or see no chance of getting their concerns met. Withdrawal is usually interpreted as agreement, and it can negatively affect your relationship with others who expect you to act.

5. *Accommodating* (aka *smoothing*): People who are accommodating are highly cooperative but unassertive. They accommodate the concerns of other people first of all, rather than their own concerns. This approach may be appropriate when the issue isn't as important to you as it is to others or when you have no choice. However, if your opponent is aggressive, accommodating may hurt your confidence. Even worse, your opponent may constantly try to take advantage of your tendency toward accommodating/smoothing.

I believe the Executive Administrator of this volunteer board could have benefited from an understanding of these different conflict management techniques. Instead of *competing* with committee chairs by micromanaging so many tasks, she could have been more effective by *collaborating* with them. If she had been more cooperative, I think committee chairs and board members would have been more cooperative too.

In summary, the top-level managers of your board must take their role of "peacemaker" seriously. However, if the conflict involves them, then the role of peacemaker must be assumed by someone else (e.g., Vice Chair, your legal counsel, a neutral mediator, or trained conflict resolution manager). Going without a conflict resolution policy or procedure will only exacerbate the problem. This policy should be written into your bylaws and/or become one of your Standard Operating Procedures, as discussed in this chapter. Board members should understand their roles and responsibilities, have a healthy respect for participative, democratic leadership, and understand conflict resolution techniques. Finally, I believe Sister Gwendolyn would have agreed with this expert, "Resolving conflict is impossible if you're unwilling or unable to forgive. Resolution lies in releasing the urge to punish, which can never compensate for our losses and only adds to our injury by further depleting and draining our lives."[63] The Golden Rule is worth repeating here: *Do unto others as you have them do unto you.*

---

[63] Jeanne Segal and Melinda Smith, "Conflict Resolution Skills: Building the Skills that Turn Conflicts into Opportunities," *HELPGUIDE.org: A Trusted Non-Profit Resource*, n. d., <http://www.helpguide.org/mental/eq8_conflict_resolution.htm>.

CHAPTER 9

Committees

"Any committee is only as good as the most knowledgeable, determined, and vigorous person on it. There must be somebody who provides the flame."

--Lady Bird Johnson

Lesson 9: Committee responsibilities must be clear, fair, and reasonable

Have you ever served on committees where the chairs never rolled up their sleeves? Or one committee seemed to do everything? Or worse, YOU were the person doing everything? In my experience, "do-everything committees" are just as ineffective as "do-nothing committees" for several reasons: (1) burnout is inevitable because the output cannot be sustained, (2) the skills of some volunteers are underutilized, and (3) initial enthusiasm turns into resentment. "Do-nothing committees" can have an equally devastating impact: Volunteers lose respect for the committee chair. This lack of respect leads to poor attendance, and poor attendance leads to the death of the committee.

In my experience, the most effective committees were those led by example and collaboration, not by self-promotion and delegation. Sharing committee tasks equally — including the Committee Chair — helps build teamwork and camaraderie. As a Board Chair, one of the most effective recruitment tools I ever developed was a committee signup sheet that clearly outlined the roles and responsibilities of each committee, including WHO chaired it, WHAT tasks it performed, WHEN and WHERE it met, WHY volunteers might want to join it, and HOW to sign up. If your board doesn't have a clear description of the roles and responsibilities of each committee, get on it. When committee responsibilities are clear, fair, and reasonable, everyone benefits. What's more, boosting committee membership could be your legacy to the organization!

One of the lessons Sister Gwendolyn taught me was that well-run committees are worth their weight in gold because they support and assist the board in carrying out its responsibilities — from recruiting members to organizing events and fundraising. She also liked to say, "Committees recommend; the board decides." I have used that distinction often when orienting new board members and committee chairs. However, even if your committees know what they're supposed to do, if they're not staffed by volunteers who understand and support your mission, then you're in for a bumpy ride. Dysfunctional committees, like dysfunctional boards, can have a long-lasting, negative impact on your organization.

Case 9A: Volunteering to Chair a Committee

When I volunteered to serve on the board of this organization, I wasn't sure exactly what its mission was, but I could see that it had a busy calendar of events for members. Since it had been around for over 50 years, I assumed that other businesses, like mine, had found value in membership over the years, so I joined the board. What happened to me next often happens to newbies on boards: the President appointed me to Chair the Nominating Committee! Not only had I never chaired such a committee, but I had never seen this organization's mission or bylaws. "What's the responsibility of the Nominating Committee?" I asked. "It is defined in our bylaws," said the President, "a copy of which you can get from the board's legal counsel." Thus began my bumpy ride.

Case 9B: No Committee Descriptions

If the committees on your board have no written descriptions or committee charters (see **Figure 3** for sample charter), you are likely to be wasting people's time and setting them up for frustration and failure. Committees need mission statements, structure, guidelines, and instructions. They cannot function properly without these things in place. As the saying goes, "You can't get what you want till you know what you want."[64]

To help one organization know what it wanted, I developed a list of committee descriptions called a "Committee Signup Sheet." The sheet, which was distributed to all board members, proved to be a very useful tool for letting people know which committees needed more members, what their responsibilities were, who chaired them, and how often they met. Here is one committee description for example:

Board Operations Committee – John Doe, Chair

Meets <u>once a month</u>. Creates Standard Operating Procedures (SOPs) as needed. Reviews and updates SOPs for compliance with bylaws. Continues to review bylaws to ensure the effectiveness of the document. Confers with legal counsel as needed. Responsible for nominations to and election of the Board of Directors annually, as well as nominations for honorary awards.

Here's another example for a Fundraising Committee containing a more detailed list of committee responsibilities:[65]

---

64 "You Can't Get What You Want (Till You Know What You Want)" is a single from Joe Jackson's 1984 album, *Body and Soul*, <http://en.wikipedia.org/wiki/You_Can%27t_Get_What_You_Want_%28Till_You_Know_What_You_Want%29>.

65 "Board Committee Job Descriptions," *CompassPoint Nonprofit Services,* 1999, <https://www.compasspoint.org/board-committee-job-descriptions>.

Fundraising Committee – Mary Smith, Chair

The Fundraising Committee's job is not simply to raise money. Instead, the Fundraising Committee is responsible for overseeing the organization's overall fundraising and, in particular, the fundraising done by the board. To accomplish this, its responsibilities are:

- *To work with staff to establish a fundraising plan that incorporates a series of appropriate vehicles, such as special events, direct mail, product sales, etc.*
- *To work with fundraising staff in their efforts to raise money*
- *To take the lead in certain types of outreach efforts, such as chairing a dinner/dance committee or hosting fundraising parties, etc.*
- *To be responsible for involvement of all board members in fundraising, such as having board members make telephone calls to ask for support, and*
- *To monitor fundraising efforts to be sure that ethical practices are in place, that donors are acknowledged appropriately, and that fundraising efforts are cost effective.*

Once you have job descriptions for all your committees, you need to ask board members to sign up. I recommend including your committee descriptions in their orientation packet. Experience has taught me that new board members are more likely to get involved on committees if you create a comprehensive orientation program — with meetings, introductions to key people, and good information to read (e.g., mission, bylaws, org chart, board meeting dates, background on the organization, last annual report, newsletters, minutes, committee descriptions, and contact information for key people on the board). New board members need information, but they often don't know what information to ask for. Introduce them to the material listed above.

Finally, one of the best ways to get board members involved on committees is to pair them up with an experienced board member who is willing to answer questions, take phone calls, and generally provide a helping hand until the "newbie" becomes established and feels comfortable on your board.

Case 9C: No Committee Recruitment Strategy

Successful boards, like successful committees, should be made up of individuals with skills in a specific area and a commitment to your mission. The problem I experienced on this board was that it had no strategy for recruiting board members, nor did it have a strategy for recruiting committee members. Getting anyone to serve on its board was a challenge every year, and getting them to serve on committees was even harder. Sound familiar?

If your board is having trouble getting people to serve on committees, ask your President to invite new board members *personally* to serve on at least one committee and/or to be the President's guest at one meeting to check it out. I can tell you from experience that people who are asked by their President to serve on a specific committee aren't likely to refuse. Most board members just need to (and often prefer to) be asked. Here are some suggestions to help with recruitment.

First, explain to prospective members that they could be instrumental in helping to overhaul the board or solve an important problem (be specific). If appropriate, let them know that they would be working with a task force of like-minded board members who are committed to making the board work. Tell them when the task force would meet (be specific). Be personal in your appeal by asking, "Would you work with me on that task force?"

Second, if board nominations are due in November, start recruiting in July, or at least four months in advance of the election. If you wait until September, the clock could run out and you could be left with very few options. Start recruiting by promoting from within your ranks. Try to match the needs and requirements of the committee with the skills and interests of prospective committee members. Your Executive Administrator may know best who the "worker bees" are and who would make a good board member or committee member. Ask him or her for recommendations. Volunteers, clients, and donors are good candidates because they are already familiar with your organization.

Third, if that still doesn't work, form a short-term Recruiting Task Force that could help identify and recommend prospective board members. Or, if you don't already have one, you could establish a Governance Committee with the following job description, for example:

As a general rule, the Governance Committee handles board recruitment, orientation, self-assessment, continuing education, and management. Recruitment involves identifying current and projected vacancies on the board, assessing the composition of the current board and identifying gaps in competencies or demographics, and finding and recruiting potential board members. The Governance Committee is charged with developing a position description for board membership to inform prospective candidates of the organization's expectations in terms of their experience and background and what will be expected of them if they join the board. The Governance Committee can also serve as the Nominating Committee for new board members and officers.[66]

Fourth, if you still need more volunteers on your board or committees, then put a "Volunteer Wanted" announcement in your newsletter or local newspaper. Include the time commitment and qualifications you are seeking for this board or committee volunteer. One of the recruitment strategies that worked for this volunteer board was the "Committee Signup Sheet" that was distributed to new board members, at new member orientation, and at the group's annual meeting. The advantage of distributing it at the annual meeting was that every member had a chance to meet every committee chair, ask questions, and take it home to read. It gave them the time and information required to make informed decisions about what, if any, committee they wanted to join.

Case 9D: Too Many Chiefs and Not Enough Indians

A committee with too many chiefs and not enough Indians isn't likely to get much done, nor is it likely to last very long. Likewise, no one likes to belong to a committee where one or two people do all the work and the others delegate but seldom roll up their sleeves. I can tell you from experience on one board that when people are used to calling the shots in their own businesses, they often find it difficult to shift roles and take direction from a committee chair. The challenge for the committee chair is

---

[66] Eileen Morgan Johnson, "Board Committee Structure, *ASAE: The Center for Association Leadership,*" January 2006, <http://www.asaecenter.org/Resources/whitepaperdetail.cfm?ItemNumber=24191>.

to understand the skills and abilities of the members and then match them with clear, fair, and reasonable responsibilities.

As Lady Bird Johnson so aptly put it, "Any committee is only as good as the most knowledgeable, determined, and vigorous person on it. There must be somebody who provides the flame." Having too many chiefs (i.e., too many flames) is likely to "ignite" the group and turn meetings into a hot mess. The committee chair must assume responsibility for setting agendas, calling meetings, preparing and presenting committee reports, and facilitating conflict resolution. In short, every committee needs one "chief" who sets the tone and drives committee goals forward. What should this tone be? According to one source:

> A good facilitator or leader knows they cannot commandeer the meeting and cannot allow others to do so. The leader senses where the group is at odds and keeps people in check and on track. Strong leaders always produce better results — but *inclusive* leadership works even better. An individual who can motivate and move people to perform to the best of their ability is extremely powerful.[67]

How can you get people to perform to the best of their ability? As President of this board, I made a point of meeting privately with every committee chair and attending a few of their meetings to see how they were doing and to thank them publicly for their leadership. To continue the dialogue, I also instituted quarterly meetings with all chairs at a local coffee shop. A common question of these chairs was how to know when they should step in and take charge and when to step back and listen. My advice was this: If the majority of members are favor of an issue, then you need to agree to that item and move on. I'm also a believer in impromptu straw polls to help the group see if there is enough support for an idea to devote more meeting time to it, and (when not a secret ballot) for the attendees to see who is on which side of a question. In this way everyone in the room can see if the majority of members favor an issue or not, before they actually have to vote on it.

---

[67] Hillary Pember, "Secrets of Successful Committees: Clarity is Key," *The Cooperator*, 2014, <http://cooperator.com/articles/2089/1/Secrets-of-Successful-Committees/Page1.html>.

Case 9E: Lack of Commitment — Committees with Nothing to Report

Whenever a committee chair is called on to report and says, "I have nothing to report," what do you think? Clearly, this is a red flag that nothing has been done. Now I wonder: why would someone chair a committee that does nothing? I believe the lack of committee participation can have several underlying causes including: (1) The members were appointed for the wrong reason (e.g., as a favor to a friend or for political reasons) and may not have been committed fully to the goals of the committee. (2) The committees had no job descriptions or charters so members didn't know what they were supposed to do, and lacking a clear purpose, they did nothing. Unfortunately, because the skills of volunteers were underutilized, they stopped coming to meetings, and poor attendance eventually led to the death of the committee. (3) The committees had no orientation so they didn't know how the committees worked, who would benefit, or even what they would get out of it.

Since Executive Administrators generally are salaried employees and not voting members of the board, it is highly inappropriate for them to appoint anyone to a committee. In so doing, they are would be usurping the authority of the President and, ultimately, the board who really should approve all committee appointments. Every committee should have a written job description or charter so members understand their roles and responsibilities. Third, someone in your organization should provide an orientation for all new committee chairs and new committee members at least once a year. If arranging an orientation is a problem, then at least schedule a conference call to go over essentials. Whatever arrangement you choose, make sure the trainer explains the purpose of each committee, how it works, who will benefit, and the benefits they can expect from serving on this committee.

Case 9F: Lack of Fairness — One or Two Committees Doing Everything

Even the best-run committees will have conflicts, but inequity or unfair treatment is one issue that really pushes people's buttons. Why? Because when people feel they are shouldering most of the workload, they generally feel unappreciated too. They become disenchanted with the process, question the mission, and wonder why they volunteered in the first place! Indeed, this was my experience while serving on a volunteer board. One or two committees seemed to be doing everything, while other committees had nothing to report and seldom, if ever, met. Burnout on the "do-everything" committees was inevitable because the output could not be sustained and worse, initial enthusiasm turned into resentment, mostly for the "do-nothing" committees.

The solution to this problem is similar to the one above. First, to equalize the workload, every committee needs a clearly defined job description or charter (see **Figure 3**). Second, open and honest communication helps committee members feel they are playing an important and equal part. To do this, the President and Executive Administrator must communicate their expectations clearly and must manage the workload by limiting the number of responsibilities, appointing subcommittees if appropriate, setting up a task force to complete a particular task in a few months, or creating an advisory council if appropriate. Third, the organization must resist the temptation to "form another committee" whenever a new task is required or so all board members can serve on a committee. As a general rule, board members shouldn't serve on more than two committees at a time. Why not? I agree with this answer: "Limiting service to one committee gives the board members the opportunity to really focus on an area and develop some expertise that can further the work of the organization."[68]

Case 9G: Lack of Structure — Poorly Run Meetings

Successful committees have well-run meetings. Unfortunately, we've all experienced too many poorly run, poorly structured committee meetings. My experience with one volunteer board was that some committees were too large, meeting agendas were way too long, committee reports didn't include action items, and the board didn't hold committee chairs accountable — all reasons why so many volunteer boards and committees fall apart.

Successful committees typically have an assigned chairperson and no more than five members, thereby avoiding the risk of "analysis paralysis" where a decision or action is stalled or never taken because the group

---

[68] Johnson.

presents too many detailed options.[69] If your board has 25 members, then a structure of five standing committees should be sufficient (e.g., Executive Committee, Governance, Finance/Audit Committee, Membership, and Program). Other ad hoc committees for your board might include Bylaws, Capital Campaign, and Strategic Planning, for example. There are no hard and fast guidelines as to how many committees are too many or not enough on a volunteer board. Successful boards create committees, task forces, and advisory councils based on the organization's needs — with the intention of dividing the workload and expertise efficiently and fairly.

If your meeting agendas are too long, try creating (or downloading) an agenda template to help you limit the number of agenda items and set time limits for presenters. You can find a variety of these on the Internet or even in Microsoft Word. Put the most important topics first to allow time for discussion, then stop the meeting at the scheduled time so even if you haven't covered everything, the least important items will be the last ones cut. Although written reports should be expected from every board committee, committee reports should be brief, emphasizing the committee's recommendations, action items, deadlines for completion, and next steps. What are the signs of a good committee functioning well? For a succinct list, see **Figure 8**.

---

[69] "Analysis Paralysis," *Wikipedia*, 24 July 2014, <http://en.wikipedia.org/wiki/Analysis_paralysis>.

Signs of a Good Committee Functioning Well

- Purpose of the committee is clear to all
- Careful time control: length of meetings, as well as development of overall committee time path
- Sensitivity within to each other's needs; good communication among all members
- An informal relaxed atmosphere
- Good preparation on part of the chair and members
- Interested, committed members
- Minutes are complete and concise
- Periodic self-assessment of committee's performance
- Recognition and appreciation are given to members so that they feel they are really making a contribution.
- The work of the committee is accepted and makes a valuable contribution to the organization.

Source: The Grinspoon Institute for Jewish Philanthropy[82]

Figure 8. Signs of a Good Committee Functioning Well

As I mentioned, your organization's Executive Administrator (or designee) should be responsible for training the committee chairs on how to conduct well-run meetings and how to develop a committee charter. And, once these volunteer chairs have been trained, the President should hold each leader accountable for carrying out the responsibilities of the committee and supporting your mission. If committee chairs aren't held accountable for poorly run meetings, then don't be surprised if attendance drops off at their meetings. No one enjoys unproductive meetings. No one wants their time wasted. Sometimes ABSENCE speaks louder than words.

In summary, committees are as effective (or ineffective) as the person who leads them, so it is critical that the committee chair be well trained and have all the tools necessary for success, including a commitment to your mission, a written job description, committee charter, and an

---

[70] "Thoughts on Great Committees," Grinspoon *Institute for Jewish Philanthropy: A Program of the Harold Grinspoon Foundation, n. d., p. 1,* <http://www.jcamp180.org/uploadDocs/3/Jill-Paul-Board-Committees.pdf>.

understanding of how to structure and lead good meetings. Having chaired many volunteer committees, I know how uncomfortable it feels to be doing more than my share of the work while others did little or nothing. At the same time, I've also experienced the joy of working alongside like-minded volunteers and mentors, such as Sister Gwendolyn, who freely shared their talents and time, working long hours with no pay.

If you want volunteers to continue to donate their time, then you must foster a positive, collaborative environment and not make their lives more difficult or complicated. You must also be certain that your volunteers understand the importance of sharing the workload, meeting deadlines, and supporting the mission and vision of your organization. In short, "A committee with a clearly stated mission and goal, which enlists a small set of committed and equally empowered individuals, is an effective and powerful tool for any board."[71]

---

[71]   Pember.

CHAPTER 10

Feedback

"If you don't get feedback from your performers and your audience, you're going to be working in a vacuum."

--Peter Maxwell Davies

Lesson 10: Boards must invite feedback to improve performance

The late Ed Koch, outspoken Mayor of NYC from 1978-1989, was famous for his question, "How am I doing?" Every board should be asking a similar question, "How are we doing?" Unfortunately, most boards have no formal or informal reporting mechanism. Neither do most boards have a way to share past experiences with present volunteer s— experiences that could spare them from making the same mistakes. Instead, the same issues keep recurring, and the same conflicts often go unresolved from one term to the next.

To be effective, your board needs a way to gather feedback, seek advice from others, reflect on it, and make improvements. Poor attendance at board meetings, for example, is a red flag, and you definitely should be asking the question, "How are we doing?" To begin, I recommend meeting with some of your past and present board members to share their experiences. Using their feedback and suggestions, develop a "Board Improvement Strategy" with measurable objectives, action steps, and a timeline. The time you spend actively listening to experienced board members — and finding ways to help improve performance — may be the single most important thing you do to prevent your volunteer board from falling apart.

If Sister Gwendolyn were alive, I think she would be pleased to see that the U-Mary alumni surveys that she pioneered are still being done today. In fact, just recently, I received this email, from the U-Mary Alumni Office, requesting feedback on a proposed capital campaign:

Greetings!

In response to the University of Mary's amazing growth, the University is now exploring the major components of a large capital campaign to meet the needs of future generations of U-Mary students.

The University of Mary continues to be deeply committed to meeting the needs of people of this region and beyond through the Benedictine values and servant leadership ideals that the university was founded on.

We welcome your feedback and opinions as a very important contribution to this growth plan. Please click below to take this vital and anonymous survey. Help make a difference for ongoing generations of U-Mary students. Be heard!

https://www.surveymonkey.com/s/FFF5LNK

Asking for feedback from your members, current board members, retiring board members, and your salaried employees should become a standard operating procedure for every volunteer organization. Unfortunately, feedback is seldom sought and rarely solicited by most volunteer boards.

Case 10A: The Importance of Listening and Responding

When I volunteered to serve on the board of this volunteer organization, I discovered that it didn't invite feedback of any kind from its members, nor did many volunteers attend meetings. Despite the lack of involvement, I believed strongly in its mission and wanted to help the youth in my community, so I agreed to serve as Vice President. Filled with enthusiasm and fresh ideas, I truly believed I could be a kind of "spark plug" and help move the organization forward. The sad truth was that my "revitalization" efforts (which was the name I gave my initiative) could not change a thing. Here are some reasons why.

Case 10B: Apathy

If board members aren't coming to meetings, you've got to find out why. The problem with this volunteer board was that no one was asking why. In fact, after years of apathy, the President didn't even send out meeting agendas anymore. The secretary didn't send out minutes either. In short, no one was communicating with anyone about anything!

If this sounds familiar, I recommend that you ask for a copy of the last meeting agenda and try to figure out what's been going on. You've got to communicate on a regular basis with your board members, including sending out the agenda and minutes.

Second, prepare a set of brief questions you would like to ask the board to find out why they're not coming to meetings. If your meetings are too long or are a waste of time, it's no wonder people don't attend. **Figure 9** provides five short questions, for example.

Sample Board Survey: Meetings

1. Enclosed is the agenda from the last board meeting. What, if anything, would you like to change about our meeting agendas?
2. How long should our meetings be?
3. What days/times are optimal for you?
4. What could we do to improve our board meetings?
5. If we implemented your suggestions, would you attend more board meetings? Why or why not?

Thank you for participating in this survey. Your comments are important to us.
Your Name: _____ Your Phone: _____

Figure 9. Sample Survey Regarding Board Meetings

Third, email your survey questions to your board colleagues. If they don't reply, try following up with personal phone calls. Sometimes speaking to members directly can be more effective than communicating in writing.

Fourth, present your findings to the board. Just inviting board members to participate in a survey may give them an opportunity to do (or say) something they've been waiting to do (or say) for a long time.

Case 10C: Lack of Communication and Fear of Feedback

Lack of communication and fear of feedback had paralyzed this volunteer board over the years. No one wanted to donate more time to do anything, yet alone write a survey and follow-up with phone calls. So, despite the lack of support, I accepted the challenge. I was committed to listening to our volunteers, respecting their opinions, and responding to them. Without a response, I knew they would not feel heard. And, I truly wanted everyone to feel heard.

I began my communication campaign with a survey. **Figure 10** contains the questions I developed for this volunteer board.

Sample Board Survey

1. How does this organization listen to its VOLUNTEERS?
2. What action steps could this organization take to be better listeners to ideas, comments, and suggestions of board members/VOLUNTEERS?
3. How does this organization listen to PARENTS of our members/youth?
4. What action steps could this organization take to be better listeners to PARENTS?
5. How does this organization listen to its MEMBERS/YOUTH?
6. What action steps could this organization take to be better listeners to MEMBERS/YOUTH?

Comments: Are there any other comments that you'd like to make, or that you didn't get a chance make? If so, please add them below.
Your Name: _____ Your Phone: _____

Figure 10. Sample Board Survey

Figure 11 contains a report of survey results and priorities, based on the number of people who responded to the question. That number is indicated in parentheses.

Survey Results: Top 10 Priorities
1. Send a letter to PARENTS with a checklist of tasks needed and amount of time required. (8)
2. Develop a web page of FAQs for new VOLUNTEERS, plus a packet of important info. (6)
3. Create a VOLUNTEERS' hotline listing whom to contact to get help when needed. (6)
4. Create a website with a "feedback" page for MEMBERS/YOUTH. (5)
5. Involve PARENTS in the organization in as many ways as possible. (5)
6. Give MEMBERS/YOUTH the incentive to attend club meetings by making meetings more interesting. (4)
7. Develop new club formats, such as neighborhood clubs for MEMBERS/YOUTH. (4)
8. Ask VOLUNTEERS more often for their feedback, comments, and suggestions for improvement. (4)
9. Develop board meeting agendas that offer a chance to tackle relevant issues. (4)
10. Identify best practices going on in more popular clubs and implement them in other clubs. (4)

Figure 11. Survey Results Showing Top 10 Priorities

Despite the hours and effort I devoted to developing the survey, tabulating the results, and identifying the priorities, this organization chose to do nothing with the survey results. What lesson did I learn? Before you undertake a board survey of any type, be 100% certain that your board members are committed to taking action once they get feedback, or you will be wasting your time. Without the active support of the President and the board, your efforts will be futile. An apathetic board that turns a deaf ear to feedback is going nowhere fast! What should you do? I recommend that you cut your losses and devote your time and talent elsewhere.

Case 10D: No Policy or Procedure for Getting Feedback

At the time I joined another volunteer board the outgoing President had wisely begun to develop Standard Operating Procedures (SOPs) for important tasks; namely, board meetings and elections. Because these

SOPs proved extremely helpful, I followed his lead in developing a few more during my term, including an SOP for soliciting bids from vendors and evaluating the work performance of the salaried employees. However, my term ended before we could get an SOP developed for getting feedback from exiting board members and non-renewing members, something I wish I could have done. Does your organization have a policy and procedure for interviewing outgoing board members? If not, you are missing a tremendous opportunity for strengthening your organization.

When terms end for dedicated board members or they resign, we often thank them for their service, give them a plaque, and wish them well. As evidence, I have a collection of such trophies in my office. Although I cherish them all, I also understand that I could have made an even greater contribution if I had been asked for my feedback during an exit interview. Since one of these volunteer boards had a Governance Committee, it already had a group to oversee the exit process. All it needed was a neutral third-party person to conduct the interviews. The problem was that it had no interest in or procedure for getting feedback from its outgoing, most experienced board members. Like most boards, it simply awarded plaques and wished them well, thereby missing a "golden" opportunity for improving the organization.

If your board has been turning board members out to pasture lately, I recommend that you add a critical step before you open the gate: implement a simple procedure for getting their feedback before they leave — a procedure that includes an exit interview. **Table 14** contains an example of what I mean.[72] Feel free to adapt it for your organization.

---

[72] Adapted from "Sample Exit Interview Policy/Procedure #1," *Employers Association,* December 2008, <http://www.employersassociation.com/documents/SampleExit InterviewPolicyandProcedure1.pdf>.

Table 14. Sample SOP for Board Member Exit Interviews

Section	Description
Policy	It is the policy of this organization to value, respect, and appropriately acknowledge the volunteerism of all departing board members and to elicit valuable information regarding their experience as a member of the board.
Purpose	The purpose of this policy is to identify workplace, organizational, or human resources factors that have contributed to a board member's decision to leave, thereby enabling the board to identify any trends requiring attention or any opportunities for improving the organization, to improve our ability to respond to issues; and to allow the board to improve and continue to develop recruitment and retention strategies aimed at addressing these issues.
Scope	This policy applies to all departing board members.
Procedure for Exit Interviews	A neutral, third-party representative (designated by the Governance Committee) will conduct a face-to-face exit interview with each departing board member, once the departure date has been confirmed. **Procedure to face-to-face exit interviews:** The designated representative will contact the board member in writing, inviting him/her to attend an exit interview at a mutually convenient time. The exit interview will last about 30-60 minutes, and should take place as soon as possible after the board receives the effective resignation date. The departing board member will be asked a standard set of questions and given a chance to discuss any concerns of information they feel would be beneficial for the company to know about their experience on the board. If a departing board member chooses not to participate in an exit interview, then he/she will be encouraged to complete an *Exit Interview Questionnaire*.

Section	Description
	Procedure for electronically conducted exit interviews: To ensure anonymity of the electronic exit interview process, departing board members will be assigned individual access codes in order to access the Internet-based *Exit Interview Questionnaire*. All access codes will be assigned by the Governance Committee chair and will be kept confidential. To increase the percentage of participation in exit interview surveys, the board will offer each respondent a $20 gift card incentive.
Voluntary Participation	Board members are responsible for participating in the exit interview process on a voluntary basis. Participants will be encouraged to be honest, candid, and constructive in their responses. If there are comments that the participant does not want to discuss or to be recorded, they will be given the option to include or not.
Confidentiality	The information received through exit interviews will be confidential. No specific information that could possibly be traced back to an ex-board member will be disseminated or discussed.
Reporting	The information will be analyzed regularly by the Governance Committee to identify areas or determine trends that may need to be addressed. Periodically, the committee will share their analysis and recommendations with designated members of the staff and/or the Board of Directors. The analysis and review will include the following: • Appropriate statistical information regarding the number and distribution of board member departures during the preceding year and reasons for leaving; • An analysis and discussion of any trends or common themes which are suggested by the exit interview feedback; • A summary of any actions or interventions taken during the year on the basis of exit interview information; and • Any actions the board feels are required in order to address any concerns or opportunities identified through exit interview feedback.

I believe that the individual, impressionistic comments obtained from exit interviews can be extremely insightful and useful for developing a board improvement strategy. For exit interviews to be most effective, though, you need to interview ALL departing board members so you can identify trends that point to chronic or systemic weaknesses in the organization. For this reason, it is important to design effective exit-interview protocols and administer them consistently. Don't simply file away exit-interview responses with the board member's profile, to be used only if litigation looms later. To help strengthen your volunteer board, it is vital to track these answers, look for long-term trends, and take action to build on areas in which your board excels, to help correct mistakes, and to identify opportunities to be more successful.

Case 10E: No Exit Interviews for Board Members

In general, departing board members have nothing to lose by being totally honest about their reasons for leaving, their experiences with fellow board members, or their opinions on board policy. One thing a departing board member may worry about, however, is damaging relationships that extend beyond their term of office. Some departing members may plan to stay in touch with current board members and don't want to burn bridges. Others simply don't feel comfortable bad-mouthing the people they will leave behind. For this reason, you should also give respondents the option to answer a certain question or not during an exit interview. Having no exit procedure at all is never a good way to sever board relationships because it can be interpreted as a lack of appreciation for years of dedication and service to the organization. I'd like to recommend a more humane approach.

First, develop an SOP for exiting board members, as illustrated in **Table 14**. Second, develop a list of exit interview questions to find out where your board excels and where you could use improvement. **Table 15** provides questions that can be adapted for your board.[73] These questions are not in any sequential order and include many more questions than you would normally ask in a typical exit interview. Third, when you contact departing board members, you should inform them about the purpose of

---

[73] Adapted from "White Papers: Employee Satisfaction Survey," *HR World*, 2014, <http://www.hrworld.com/whitepaper/employee-satisfaction-survey/>.

the exit interview, who will be conducting it (a neutral third party), how the information will be used, and who will have access to it.[74]

I recommend meeting in a home or office that is private as opposed to a busy restaurant or coffee shop where your conversation could be overheard. Choose the questions that are most relevant to the situation, the interviewee, and your organization. For consistency in reporting, use the same questions for every exit interview. Finally, all questions should be optional. If there are comments that participants don't want to discuss, they should be given the option.

Table 15. Sample Exit Interview Questions for Board Members

Interview Topic	Question
Your Invitation	**When you were originally approached about serving on this board was it in the context of your "goodness of fit" with mission or strategic plan?** That is, was it apparent that your professional expertise and/or your community history, relationships, capacities, and activities were being sought?
	Were you solicited for a specific organizational slot on this board? For example to serve on a specific committee or lead a particular initiative?
Reason for Serving	**Why did you originally agree to serve on this board?**
Orientation & Training	**Before or just after your induction, was there an orientation session for new board members?** In retrospect, how useful was the orientation? In what specific ways might it have been better?
	Did you receive enough training and support while serving on this board? If not, how could it have been better?

---

[74] Jill Geddes, "Why Are Exit Interviews Important?" *Trillium Teams,* 2014, <http://www.trilliumteams.com/articles/23/why-are-exit-interviews-important?->.

Interview Topic	Question
Expectations	**Were the organizational expectations made completely clear to you?** For example, was it conveyed that attendance at full-board and committee meetings was a minimum expectation, and that, beyond this minimum, you would be expected to attend other board-related functions?
	Were the financial expectations made just as clear? That is, was it made clear that board members were expected to give or pledge first in advance of every fund-raising activity, whether annual giving or major capital campaigns?
	Was your understanding about the requirements of serving consistent with your actual board experience?
	Did you feel the expectations of you as a board member were realistic? If not, why not?
Your Role	**Did you feel comfortable and confident in participating in full-board discussions from the start?** Why or why not?
	Did you feel your perspective was listened to and respected?
	Were your talents and background used appropriately from the start? Can you offer an example?
	Did you move immediately into a committee role in which you felt at home?
	As your tenure on the board progressed, were you utilized in ways that reflected your increasing understanding of your role? How?

Interview Topic	Question
Reasons for Leaving	What made you decide to leave this board? Were you frustrated with some issues, or was there an external reason to leave, such as a spouse relocating? What are your feelings about leaving the board? What would it have taken for you to stay?
Likes	What did you like best about serving on this board? What was most enjoyable or satisfying for you in your time with us?
Dislikes	What did you find least satisfying about serving on this board? What was most frustrating, difficult, or upsetting to you in your time with us?
Challenges	What were the biggest challenges to you in performing your board responsibilities?
Board & Staff	What could the board or staff have done to improve your experience?
Level of Support	How would you rate the level of support you received to perform your duties on this board? What could you have done better or more for us had we given you the opportunity?
Policies & Procedures	Did any board policies or procedures inhibit you from performing your duties to the best of your ability? What, if any, examples of ridiculous policy, rules, instructions, can you highlight?

Interview Topic	Question
Board Operations	How do you think this board as a whole functions?
	What suggestions would you make for improving the way the board operates?
	What improvements to meetings or structure would you suggest?
Strategic Planning	Was a strategic or long-range planning process undertaken during your time on the Board? If so, please comment on both process and outcome.
Board Meetings	Did the full-board meetings seem purposeful from the start?
	Were the meetings clearly focused upon committee proposals for action? Did they seem well-led, purposeful, and appropriate in length?
	How would you change the Board meetings to improve effectiveness?
Committees	Did committee meetings seem purposeful? Appropriate in length? Well-led?
	How would you improve these meetings?
Feedback	What kind of performance feedback did you receive and how regularly?
Qualities for Success	What qualities and characteristics do you think a person should have to be successful in this organization?
Advice to Incoming Board Members	What advice would you offer incoming board members?
Future Projects	What is the single most important project or process the board should next undertake?
Self-Assessment	If you could do the job over again what would you do differently?

Interview Topic	Question
Future Contact	What can we do to enable you to pass on as much of your knowledge and experience as possible to your replacement/successor prior to your departure? If I can call you in the future, what issue should I consult you about?
Overall Board Experience	How would you describe your overall board experience? Thinking back over your entire time of service, in what area does it seem the board excelled most? Failed to succeed most?

You will get the best responses to your exit questions by being positive, constructive, understanding, and helpful during the exit interview process. Be an active listener, don't be defensive. Follow-up the interview with a thank you note, not only for this volunteer's board service, but also for the time spent in debriefing. As Sister Gwendolyn would say, "If you treat people with integrity and decency, generally they will respond in kind."

In conclusion, healthy boards continuously strive to add value to the organization, and getting feedback is essential tool for helping you find ways to add value. "Working in a vacuum" as Peter Maxwell Davies says, doesn't work for performers and their audience. Neither does it work for volunteer boards. To add real value to your organization, you need to solicit feedback from current members, officers, staff, board members, and departing board members too. In my experience, apathy, fear of feedback, and lack of exit policies and procedures have prevented many boards from maximizing the talents they've assembled. Don't ignore the comments made by exiting board members. Study them carefully. Look for patterns and trends. Improving communication through exit interviews should become a priority for your board. The time you spend actively listening to experienced board members — and finding ways to help improve performance — may be the single most important thing you do to prevent your volunteer board from falling apart.

WORKS CITED

"30 Example Vision Statements." *Top Nonprofits,* 2014. Web. 8 August 2014.

"52 Volunteer Appreciation Ideas eBook." *Baudville: The Place for Daily Recognition,* 2011. Web. 8 August 2014.

"About Conflict." *Academic Leadership Support: Office of Quality Improvement and Office of Human Resource Development,* n. d., Web. 8 August 2014.

"About U-Mary: Our Statement of Mission & Identity." *University of Mary,* n. d. Web. 8 August 2014.

"Accountability." *Merriam-Webster Dictionary,* 2014. Web. 8 August 2014.

"Accountability in Teams." *Talent Technologies,* 15 November 2012. Web. 8 August 2014.

"Alumni Association: Current Committee Members." *University of Mary,* n. d. Web. 8 August 2014.

"Alumni Association: Former Council Members." *University of Mary,* n. d. Web. 8 August 2014.

"Analysis Paralysis." *Wikipedia,* 24 July 2014. Web. 8 August 2014.

"Authoritarian Leadership," *Business Dictionary.com,* 2014. Web. 8 August 2014.

"Authoritarian Leadership Style," *Wikipedia,* 25 February 2014. Web. 8 August 2014.

"Best Examples of a Vision Statement." *Your Dictionary,* 2014. Web. 8 August 2014.

"Board Committee Job Descriptions." *CompassPoint Nonprofit Services,* 1999. Web. 8 August 2014.

"Chapter 3: Summoning the Brothers for Counsel." *The Rule of St. Benedict in English.* Ed. Timothy Fry, OSB, et al. Collegeville, MN: The Liturgical Press, 1982. Print.

"Chapter 64: The Election of an Abbot." *The Rule of St. Benedict in English.* Ed. Timothy Fry et al. Collegeville, MN: The Liturgical Press, 1982. Print.

Cullinane, Mollie. "Nonprofit Law Basics: Can the Executive Director Serve on the Board of Directors?" *Cullinane Law Group,* 16 April 2012. Web. 8 August 2014.

Freund, Annette S. "Why Volunteer Boards Fall Apart: Ten Lessons Learned in the Trenches," 2013. Print.

Heathfield, Susan M. "Resistance to Change Definition." *About.com,* 2014. Web. 8 August 2014.

"History & Legacy." *W.K. Kellogg Foundation,* n. d. Web. 8 August 2014.

Humphrey-Pratt, Cheryl. "Volunteer Recognition: Matching Motivation to Rewards." *RCVO @ Volunteer Alberta,* 2006. Web. 8 August 2014.

Jackson, Joe. "You Can't Get What You Want (Till You Know What You Want." *Body and Soul,* 1984. Album.

Jennings, C. Alan. "A Committee of Special Standing." *Robert's Rules for Dummies.* Hoboken, NJ: Wiley Publishing, 2005. Print.

Johnson, Eileen Morgan. "Board Committee Structure, *ASAE: The Center for Association Leadership,* January 2006. Web. 8 August 2014.

Josephson, Michael. "Commentary 847.4: Moral Courage –The Engine of Integrity," *What Will Matter,* 2 October 2013. Web. 8 August 2014.

---. *Making Ethical Decisions.* Los Angeles, CA: The Josephson Institute of Ethics, 2002. Print.

Laub, Jim. "Servant Leadership: Defining Servant Leadership and the Healthy Organization." *OLAgroup,* 2014. Web. 8 August 2014.

"Leadership Styles." *Big Dog & Little Dog's Performance Juxtaposition,* 22 July 2014. Web. 8 August 2014.

Lewin, Kurt, Ronald Lippitt, and Ralph K. White. "Patterns of Aggressive Behavior in Experimentally Created 'Social Climates.'" *Journal of Social Psychology,* 10 (1939): 271-299. Print.

"Liability." *Merriam-Webster Dictionary,* 2014. Web. 8 August 2014.

"Managing Our Funds." *Make-a-wish Foundation of America,* 2014. Web. 8 August 2014.

"Managing People." *SmallBizConnect,* n. d. Web. 8 August 2014.

"Mediation in the Nonprofit Organization." *Mediate.com,* 2014. Web. 8 August 2014.

Merrill, Mary V. "Recognizing Volunteers." *World Volunteer Web,* 27 September 2005. Web. 8 August 2014.

"Mission." *Wounded Warriors*, 2013. Web. 8 August 2014.

"Mission and Vision." *Smithsonian*, n. d. Web. 8 August 2014.

"Mission Statement and Principles." *Habitat for Humanity International*, 2014. Web. 8 August 2014.

"Mission, Vision & Values." *Cleveland Clinic*, 2014. Web. 8 August 2014.

"Negativism." *The Free Dictionary*, 2014. Web. 8 August 2014.

"Our Mission: Servant Leadership at U-Mary." *University of Mary*, n. d. Web. 8 August 2014.

"Our Vision, Mission & Values." *Save the Children*, 2014. Web. 8 August 2014.

Overfield, Darren and Rob Kaiser. "One Out of Every Two Managers is Terrible at Accountability," *Harvard Business Review,* 8 November 2012. Web. 8 August 2014.

Pember, Hillary. "Secrets of Successful Committees: Clarity is Key." *The Cooperator*, 2014. Web. 8 August 2014.

"Philosophy." *Special Olympics*, n. d. Web. 8 August 2014.

Pirtle, Connie. "Ask Connie: All Things Recognition." *Volunteer Today.com: The Complete Gazette for Volunteerism*, 2014. Web. 8 August 2014.

"Prologue." *The Rule of St. Benedict in English.* Ed. Timothy Fry et al. Collegeville, MN: The Liturgical Press, 1982. Print.

"The Psychology of Bullying." *Theravive,* 2014. Web. 8 August 2014.

"Rigidity." *The Free Dictionary*, 2014. Web. 8 August 2014.

Robert, Henry M. et al. "Improper Motions." *Roberts Rules of Order Newly Revised.* 10th ed. Cambridge, MA: Da Capo Press, 2000. Print.

"Sample Advisory Committee Charter: Charter for Agricultural Advisory Committee." *Program Planning Handbook* Colombia, MO: University of Missouri, n. d. Web. 8 August 2014.

"Sample Exit Interview Policy/Procedure #1." *Employers Association.* December 2008. Web. 8 August 2014.

"Santayana Quotations." *Indiana University School of Liberal Arts*, 2011. Web. 8 August 2014.

Segal, Jeanne and Melinda Smith. "Conflict Resolution Skills: Building the Skills that Turn Conflicts into Opportunities." *HELPGUIDE.org: A Trusted Non-Profit Resource*, n. d. Web. 8 August 2014.

Shade, Henry E. "Accountability in Leadership." *Innovision Global*, n. d. Web. 8 August 2014.

"Standard Operating Policy – Promoting a Respectful Workplace: Preventing and Managing Workplace Bullying." *Ambulance Service of New South Wales*, 18 July 2012. Web. 8 August 2014.

Sturgis, Alice. "Selecting a Nominating Committee." *The Standard Code of Parliamentary Procedure*. 4th ed. New York: McGraw-Hill, 1966. Print.

Thomas, Kenneth and Ralph H. Kilmann. "An Overview of the Thomas-Kilmann Conflict Mode Instrument." *Kilmann Diagnostics: Dedicated to Resolving Conflict throughout the World*, 2014. Web. 8 August 2014.

"Thoughts on Great Committees." *Grinspoon Institute for Jewish Philanthropy: A Program of the Harold Grinspoon Foundation*, n. d. Web. 8 August 2014.

"Traditionalism." *The Free Dictionary*, 2014. Web. 8 August 2014.

"Training Module 5: Part B, The Board of Directors – Recruitment, Training & Effectiveness." *Southern Early Childhood Association*, n. d. Web. 8 August 2014.

"Turf War." *Macmillan Dictionary*, 2014. Web. 8 August 2014.

"Turf War." *The Free Dictionary*, 2014. Web. 8 August 2014.

"Types of Conflict." *Conflict Resolution, Definition of Conflict, Conflict Management Styles*, n. d. Web. 8 August 2014.

"Who We Are." *Amnesty International*, 2014. Web. 8 August 2014.

"A World Free of MS." *National Multiple Sclerosis Society*, n. d. Web. 8 August 2014.